OPEN
MIND TO
CHANGE

A Guidebook to the Great Awakening

MARTIN GEDDES

Open Your Mind to Change: A Guidebook to the Great Awakening

ISBN: 978-1-7363937-3-4

Third Imprint, December 2021.
Second Imprint banned by Barnes & Noble on October 30, 2021.
First Imprint banned by Amazon on April 29, 2021.

Foreword by Robert David Steele.
Edited by Shelley Allen.
Cover design by Matthew James Lawler.
Author photograph by Chris George.

Martin Geddes
Open Minds Media
London, England
contact@openmindschange.com
openmindschange.com

Narrated edition available at openmindschange.com/audiobook.

Contents

Foreword

by Robert David Steele

I FIRST BECAME AWARE OF MARTIN GEDDES after I overcame my skepticism with respect to the Q phenomenon and the related Anons. These are two different groups of people, one official and small, the other much larger and volunteer in nature.

There were three major influences upon me when the time came for me to appreciate the wit and wisdom and deep integrity and intelligence of Martin Geddes:

First, I have known Mike Flynn personally since 2014. While we have never discussed Q, because Mike has been enjoined from multiple forms of engagement during his imposed purgatory, it became clear to me over a year ago that Mike Flynn's fingerprints were all over Q. Q is, as my CWO-4 mentor from my time in Afghanistan in 2013 has suggested, the single greatest information operation — for peace and in the public interest — in modern history.

Second, my own examination of Q posts and related Anons from 2017 and 2018 persuaded me in 2019 and 2020 that the factual depth and breadth of Q could not be denied. Then I met Sidney Powell and two others with direct contact with the White House, and I began to see the endgame for what Martin calls "the Silent War" that has been won by the White Hats against the Deep State. The demise of what Martin calls "pathocracy" is here, and I am seeing nothing less than Nuremberg-like trials forthcoming: not just military tribunals in the USA against US traitors, but also international trials for the combined crime against humanity known as the COVID weapon of mass destruction, weapon of mass disruption, and weapon of mass deception. The global economy has been wrecked, and society gutted, by design.

Third, and least important, have been my own experiences as a former spy and professional intelligence officer, last responsible for creating the newest national intelligence analysis capability in the USA, the Marine Corps Intelligence Activity. I have also been, by chance, the top reviewer of non-fiction books in English, with over 2,000 reviewed across 98 domains. This allows me to say with absolute conviction that all of my experience on the dark side, and all of my reading on the light side, totally validate everything that Martin Geddes is putting forward.

I have interviewed Martin Geddes on video twice; I have read his articles on Q as well as this work of aggregated short pieces from the past. Despite our both being deplatformed by the criminal media elements in service to the Deep State, I can say with some measure of confidence that his voice and his vision are easily in the top dozen among all whom I know.

Here are the highlights from this particular work that make it, in my view, absolutely essential reading for every person of conscience on the Earth:

1. He opens with remarks on **ponerology** — the study of evil and its underlying psychopathy.
2. He connects the prevalence of evil to the rise of the **pathocracy**.
3. He outlines the manner in which **our information ecology is rigged** to support evil.
4. He appreciates that **truth is naturally self-consistent** (i.e., zero maintenance cost).
5. His optimism stems in part from the raw fact that **lies require a great deal of effort** to maintain, so they implode when faced with an alternative media ecology.
6. **The abdication of humanity to the mandarins of money is literal insanity at scale.**
7. **White hats have been laboring toward a global purge of corruption for decades.**
8. Institutionalized crime is civilian in nature — the **uniformed military is its counter-balance.**

9. The Silent War is not a political war — it is **a spiritual war seeking to restore public good.**
10. **Institutionalized fraud is being terminated**, including war, non-profits, and foreign aid.
11. **Humanity, morality, and identity are central to the public's inevitable triumph.**
12. The **loss of legitimacy across the media** — both mass and social — is the beginning of the end.
13. The **loss of legitimacy within academia** — both social and scientific — deepens the collapse of evil.
14. **Do not under-estimate the resilience and power of the human spirit.**
15. The White Hats are setting the stage for freedom — but **only you can actualize your freedom.**
16. This is at root **an information war** — a silent war with digital soldiers, memes as bullets, and social media as the machine gun.
17. **Satanic pedophilia is the "glue" for the supermafia — and it includes cannibalism.**
18. **Knowledge hoarding and deliberate myth-building** have protected the supermafia.
19. **COVID-19 is the ultimate global crime against humanity** and will bring down the supermafia.
20. **Our objective is to restore truth and virtue as the foundation for human society.**
21. **The digital coup — and our readiness to document and expose it — is the *coup de'grâce*.**
22. From the Great Exposures come not the Great Reset but **the Great Upset.**

— *Robert David Steele*

Introduction

December 20, 2020

THE SAGE AND PHILOSOPHER Jiddu Krishnamurti (1895–1986) said that "truth is a pathless land," meaning we each have our own individual journey towards seeing reality for what it is. My path is different from yours. My "jolt" of awakening, that begun my first steps on my path, was between 2011 and 2015. That was when I realized there is no possible way that the "official" story of the events of September 11, 2001, can be true.

The narrative being offered requires the laws of physics to change, and political absurdities to be taken as fact. Since you are reading this, you will already have had your own "jolt" to reject the falsehood being offered as truth. Led by different experiences and personal characters, we each construct our own model of reality. It cannot be any other way; yet a successful society requires some level of shared reality.

When Donald Trump was elected President of the United States, I did not initially grasp the significance or magnitude of this event. It took me another year or more to sense that something profound and benevolent was underway. While I knew something was deeply wrong with the world, I was optimistic about humanity's ability to turn things around. I had little clue about how bad things had been, nor how good they might become.

The first essay presented in this book was published around a week before the first "Q drop," which is a backchannel from the military to the public. As such I feel justifiably proud of my prescience. However, that does not mean I am a sage or guru who can see into the future. I am a "presentologist," not a futurologist. Any foresight is merely the result of more diligent attention to *what is* in the *now*.

I am also a "synthesist" rather than an analyst. I like to see the "big picture" rather than focus on details. This happens to also be the very thing that psychopaths wish to keep to themselves at the apex of their pyramid of control. They don't want you to "connect the dots" since their power rests on them being disconnected and compartmentalized. Derogatory terms like "conspiracy theorist" are designed to discourage inquiry into a psychopathic conspiracy against all of humanity.

Even as I write I am still learning more about my own ignorance. Until very recently I did not fully appreciate the role of the Chinese Communist Party in infiltrating and subverting the West. I did not anticipate the figural role of the 2020 election as a sting operation to draw out this enemy into the open. (This is also why my predictions on timing are consistently off, even if the direction is undeniably correct.) I did not grasp that the attempted genocide of humanity was a goal of these powerful psychopaths.

I have deliberately not written about many potentially important topics — like alien disclosure, an economic reset, or accessing higher consciousness — simply because I am not qualified to comment upon them. I am offering you cartography skills, not a finalized map. You are going to have to scope your own research, stride along your own path, and synthesize your own understanding of the world. Please take this writing as merely an exemplar of "one man and a laptop" doing his best to figure it all out.

As I write it is the evening of December 20, 2020. Tomorrow is a major celestial event — the conjunction of Saturn and Jupiter — which prospectively kicks off a period of unprecedented change in the human condition. The first term of President Trump was a case of "everything is a sting operation," and we have endured much pain in that process. The second term holds the promise of massive disclosure, justice for the hideous crimes committed, and the unification of humanity. The agony is henceforth for the criminals only.

I am pleased that the foreword is by Robert David Steele since he has a critical mantra: "The truth at any cost lowers all other costs." This cannot be over-emphasized; our "reality" has been endlessly "hacked" to divide us against each other. As our worldviews realign, our conflicts will subside.

Techniques like "open source everything" (one of his key initiatives for a better world) will "defragment" the world and level-up opportunity.

If peace is the prize, truth is the winning ticket.

— *Martin Geddes*

Why I Am Optimistic about the Future

October 21, 2017

HAVING DINNER WITH A FRIEND recently, I surprised him with my optimism and was forced to explain why. After rambling for a long time and darting down some rabbit holes, I eventually came up with something half-coherent. So here is the 75%-coherent version.

It is easy to be gloomy when the economy is shaky, the TV news is full of barbarity, and the planet is facing ecocide. The long, dark and cold nights of the northern winter are approaching, too. Melancholy and misery are sometimes comfortable companions.

Yet taking a "grand sweep" look at history, I see many reasons to be positive about the future. The negativity we presently experience is the result of the collapse of ancient and unwelcome structures of corrupt power and contrived hate.

Let me explain why you, too, might wish to adopt a more positive attitude toward what is coming and also dream of an approaching golden age that could be a great surprise to many who today face suffering.

Over the past few years, I have spent many a night puzzling over how the world works. This is partly motivated to heal a trauma of my own. My mother's conscience and free will is trapped inside a destructive cult, as were her parents in turn. What gave rise to that malignant movement?

As Jung counseled us, "Knowing your own darkness is the best method for dealing with the darknesses of other people." I've certainly spent a lot of time examining my own special madness, which is an exquisite fractal of folly. I've also taken to examining the darknesses of others.

This led me to discover... *ponerology*. No, I hadn't heard of it, either. It is the academic study of evil. Maybe we all ought to have heard of it!

Seems like it might have some bearing on our plight as conscious beings struggling for survival.

This in turn has uncovered the apparently figural role of psychopaths in society and how they are widely (and possibly intentionally) misunderstood. Those without a conscience are believed to make up 1–4% of the population, and they have an outsized influence on our institutions and culture.

Historically, it seems that psychopaths had a useful role. Their lack of fear was handy for those moments when the proverbial saber-toothed tiger strolled into the hamlet. They would also defend your seed corn from marauding tribes when there was a drought.

But you would know that it was wise to keep your sons and daughters well away from them. The seductiveness of their poisoned charm would be contained by the small-scale, social nature of group life. Their past misdeeds and proclivities for wrongdoing would be remembered and known.

The arrival of the printing press, and later mass media, bypassed our natural defenses. Psychopaths were able to express their sociopathic doctrines in book form, and a conscience-free textbook might look like any other from a normal, loving human. Their personal and family history would be remote to you, filtered through intermediaries, so you would not know why it should be ignored.

As a result of this new dynamic, the mere existence of a *Mein Kampf* on the shelf of the bookstore could legitimize its existence and spread. What's worse, the act of reading it infects you with its framing, even if you reject its factual basis and reasoning.

In a slightly inappropriate, jokey way, I refer to this as the "Vitabiotics problem." Sitting on a London tube train, imagine you see an advert with a picture of a woman with long and luscious hair. It states, "I use Vitabiotics every day. My hair is wonderful!" The astute reader promptly notices that this invites a form of false inference about the vitamin product's value.

What you haven't noticed is that the sighting of the Vitabiotics product on the underground train has already legitimized it in your mind as a product that belongs in retail stores and assigns it a similar quality and efficacy to everything else you purchase. That's how the subversive mind trick operates.

By the time you read the text, it is too late. The emotive you is influenced; the rational you arrives after the decision-maker — who operates on feelings only — has already left the conscious frame.

(Side note: I have no idea whether Vitabiotics products promote trichological triumph and have no axe to grind with them. They are clearly having to work around rules on the advertising of medicines and healthcare products, so it is wrong to accuse them of deliberate dissembling.)

We see this pattern in play every day in the media. For instance, no matter what you think of Hillary Clinton, many images of her in the media legitimize her as a public figure. The British newspaper, The Observer, for example, featured on the front page of its October 15, 2017 edition a large photograph of the former first lady bedecked in bright red, gold and black graduate regalia, robes of distinction conferred upon honorary dignitaries.

She might be a figure of hate and derision for many, but the implied suggestion is that she is an academic and not a criminal. Again, take this as a Vitabiotics learning moment, not a political polemic!

So, the arrival of the media business gave psychopaths leverage over the rest of us. This coincided with the growth of urban society, hierarchical organizations and licensed professions conferring authority. These are irresistible targets for psychopaths, since they amplify their control over others.

The result has been the rise of "pathocracy," which is the societal adoption of psychopaths' institutionalized beliefs. The process begins with the infection of trusted institutions by a few (who control recruitment) followed by an inversion of their moral value system. Such subversion occurs in all walks of life, but especially in circumstances wherein psychopaths can hold positions of great power over others. The obvious cases include politicians, military leaders and CEOs, but it also manifests in other professions, like surgeons and ministers of religion.

My sense is we are now at a place of "peak pathocracy."

Psychopaths maintain control and dominance by requiring subordinates to act in accordance with their warped intentions. Their perfect society is one in which information is compartmentalized; they are at the top of the pyramid, while the masses are herded into a hierarchy of scopes of understanding. (Look up "viable system theory" to understand why this is so.)

Those at the very top are fully "in the know" and have true intentionality, in this case for the purpose of evil. Those below are fed a false story about the purpose of their activities, and ideally are co-opted to believe that the intentions of those above them are good. After all, the greatest trick the Devil pulls is to tell us he doesn't exist. Evil must always present itself as good: normal people are hardwired to reject it.

My personal history means I am acutely tuned to psychological and emotional manipulation, since I have many decades of distressing direct experience. I treat sincere belief, group identity and enforced dogmas as having zero utility for signifying truth. Indeed, the cognitive dissonance that makes others recoil is positively attractive to me, as it signals a possible escape hatch from a hellish tomb of totalitarian thought control.

I escaped from the multi-generational family disaster of the Jehovah's Witnesses as a child because my personal experience clashed with their doctrines. I can assure you, this is the basic recipe for sanity: When someone presents you with two fingers plus two fingers and asks you to say five fingers, get counting. Insist on a recount if necessary. Trust yourself.

I have learned to minimize my exposure to pathocratic, "Vitabiotic" information systems. My aim is to maximize my direct and one-degree-removed circle of genuine, lived experience. I deliberately go out of my way to find and meet with people with widely varied life stories and tales.

Some of what I have found is extremely dark, and if you don't want to read about it, stop now.

OK... here goes...

I don't watch TV, as its hypnotic demand to control my attention is repulsive. I never read newspapers; the only factually reliable thing they publish is the page number. And I became disgusted with the movies years ago, which too often invited me to celebrate cruelty and violence.

People in fear are easier to control, and the mass media thrives on engineering fear. For the best possible fear, divide society into two artificial groups who are taught to hate each other and never question why the psychopaths are in charge.

Psychopaths want the rest of society to be afraid and divided, ready to be conquered. Forget "Tory vs Labour," "Jews vs Goyim," "Hutu vs Tutsi," "R vs D," or any other false divide of humanity into competing tribes. It is "psychopaths vs the rest," every time.

Fix that, and you've a hope of lasting peace. *Ponerology for the win!*

Now, I freely admit, I am not normal in my media diet. However, I also sense my own abnormality is becoming more common. Many people are shunning the mass media, resulting in declining viewership and readership. They no longer believe what they are told, or feel it is spiritually good for them or their families. Wise people know the only way to avoid pathocratic infection is to not look.

Instead, they are seeking out alternative (i.e., genuine) forms of information driven by non-psychopathic narratives. People are massing online and are gathering in many smaller real-world group meetings to compare experiences and learn. In other words, we normal people are starting to "swarm" against the pathocratic systems that harm us.

My strong belief is that the internet is powerfully amplifying personal experience and severely attenuating the projection of psychopathic belief systems. This reverses the process that the printing press and mass media initiated. That is a very big deal indeed and my core cause for optimism.

Social media allows us all to become global publishers of our lives and seek out like-minded others. A good example is the throng of people who have survived child sex abuse by pedophiles. *Oops, sorry, that's the pathocratic framing.* I mean to say, survivors of pedosadists who like to rape, torture and murder children as the vetting process for their evil club. Non-psychopaths can't fake this wicked act.

I warned you it was grim. But it's the pathocratic world we currently live in.

Having experienced the psychological and spiritual abuse of a cult as a child, I have a strong sense of the victims' hurt and desire for justice. It is also not that hard to tell who is a genuine victim when you have been one in your own way.

The collective victim narrative directly contradicts that of the mainstream media, who like to portray these matters as involving isolated "bad apple" individuals. It is, of course, never an institutionalized (and longstanding) "bug" in the operating system of society, entrenching pathocratic power structures. Nothing is allowed to contest the core currency of power, which is not money but legitimacy, leading to the consent of the victim to predation.

It is easier than ever to find people who question the beliefs that are handed to them in easy-to-digest form every night in the news or through lewd music videos or movies devoid of beauty. The internet has fundamentally disrupted the flow of information and power in society, and this cannot be reversed. It just presently takes a lot of time and energy (and diligence against confirmation bias) to sift through it all when you're fighting the turbulent flow of disinformation, misdirection and ridicule.

The truth, no matter how ugly, is naturally self-consistent. It requires no energy to maintain it. Lies, however, have a negative "information thermodynamic" that works against them. An old lie needs retelling and maintenance. New technology comes along, allowing fresh forensic examination of the past. The tools of machine learning — not least the search engine — naturally correct information power asymmetries that have lasted for millennia.

My hypothesis is that the turmoil we all currently witness are the death-throes of an information flow management system that is so longstanding and embedded into society we can barely perceive it. The cost of maintaining the "intentional knowledge compartments" is rising so fast that they are bursting in front of our eyes. While we may pass through a time of trauma, there is hope of a golden age at the far side, once we've fixed the wreckage left by pathocracy.

Orwell warned in 1948 of 1984. But 1984 is just a point in time. It is not necessarily a boot-stomping forever if it contradicts the fundamental forces of energy and flow of the universe. Conversely, Huxley posited a future where we were all far too comfortable to care about our manipulation and enslavement. That also is unlikely as a long-term outcome, since humans naturally seek freedom and flourishing.

I feel increasingly positive, no matter how much fear the daily news brings. While today's internet may be fragile, frustrating, and prone to mass surveillance, it is (on balance) doing us all great good. Furthermore, some of us are dreaming of a far better information infrastructure. It is possible, I suggest, to relate morals to mathematics and to create something that is ethical by design. Indeed, for the world of sensors and artificial intelligence, it is mandatory to do much better.

In the digital information world, we are God, and it is our job to capture and cage the Devil. So far, we normal humans are turning the tide on the psychopaths. There is only one conspiracy against love, and if we reject fear and stay unified, it can be defeated. Permanently.

ღ

The Great Awakening

May 13, 2018

Pain and suffering are always inevitable for a large intelligence and a deep heart. The really great men must, I think, have great sadness on earth.
— Fyodor Dostoyevsky

CAN YOU FEEL IT? There's something that is very different about the world right now. You can sense a shift, but struggle to put words to it. Old maps and ways of navigating life aren't up to the job. Competing and incompatible narratives about the nature of society are in vigorous competition. Some must collapse since reality ultimately trumps even the most sincere fantasy.

Over the past 7+ years, I have put in far more hours of research and effort into a "side project" than I have into telecoms and tech. The subject doesn't have a name, and there is no destination. If I was forced to describe it, I might choose "light and truth." What is real, which way is "up," and how can we really know? What I have discovered has forced me to reconsider many core beliefs.

There is no omnipotent fantasy of fixing the world all on my own. I just want to keep myself sane and my loved ones safe. Yet to have any impact in righting any wrongs of the world and infuse one's own life with lightness, it is necessary to engage in a Jungian exploration of the darkness of the soul and society. Confronting inner demons and outer devils is not a pleasant activity.

To a large degree, I have come to a final conclusion: evil has an *antifragile* "operating system" with longstanding psychopathic cultures, each perpetuating malignant beliefs over many generations and centuries. To make sense of the present's woes you have to retreat all the way back — to early civilizations and biblical times. Sumer, Babylon, Egypt and

Phoenicia inform the Western narrative; the prehistory of India, China and Japan equally so for the East.

The "golden thread" that unifies these, if there be one, is how technologies intermediate our natural social relationships and altruistic sharing nature. *Guns, germs, and steel:* yes, all do indeed play their part. Yet the most critical technology of all is *money*, which always implies debt (as all money is an IOU) and hence the potential for usury. When your debtor neighbor has a misfortune, do you collect his assets as collateral (leaving him destitute), or offer charity to remedy the situation?

Money represents an abstract claim on natural and labor resources and can be accumulated without the physical constraints of owning and defending those resources directly with fences and shackles. It is, in and of itself, a neutral phenomenon: what matters is how we relate to it and what boundaries we construct to limit its destructive downside. For, the societal risk is that *creation* of money is captured by mafias, who then impose a debt-based system of enslavement.

The dominance of money over today's society is so absolute that to question it appears to be an insanity. Yet when you step right back and understand its core function, the insanity is the system we live in. For, the power we assign to *central* banks and fiat currency is that of the gods, able to manipulate people and events at a whim. To know why requires us to distinguish between two categories of money creation.

The first is that of ordinary *commercial* banking. Banks do indeed create deposits out of thin air when they loan you money. This is not of itself a problem: as long as the bank is solvent, the IOUs it creates are valid claims on real resources. Even if you cannot repay your loan, the bank is on the hook to make good the IOU to anyone who redeems it. Charging interest reflects this integral insurance element of banking and is a fair reward for pricing it well.

Central banking is different. The origination of national debt, backed by the state's power to tax, does *not* imply that the central banker will personally take on the burdens of caring for the sick and poor should there be a sovereign default. Central banking comes with the additional power to initiate collapses (via credit starvation), so as to enable the bankster classes to cheaply seize assets held as collateral.

There is also the inbuilt incentive to fund wars (loaning money to both sides) and to create a parallel system of political bribery, blackmail and corruption funded using fiat money, not all of which may be on the books — the US Fed hasn't been audited for a reason. Finally, there is the temptation to inject money (and transactional relationships) into every social sphere, displacing the gift economy for which humans are neurologically hardwired.

The control that money creation offers attracts the most sociopathic elements in society since they must be entirely unempathetic to the resulting suffering of the populace. Perhaps unsurprisingly, the story of the last 6000 years is therefore the relationship between the money-changers and the temple-keepers, who *ought* to be the custodians of our collective morality. Who defines what is usury and where charity should begin and end?

A "successful" takeover of society by debt-based slavery requires voluntary servitude because force cannot scale. This means a *pathocratic* governance system that subverts natural law and human love. That in turn requires three ingredients: hierarchical structures under the cruel control of psychopaths; hidden (occult) knowledge, curated by secret societies to create persistent covert power; and processes of infiltration, infection and inversion to redirect the resources and energies of institutions, especially those of a spiritual or religious nature.

As Mark Twain quipped, "Truth is stranger than fiction, but it is because Fiction is obliged to stick to possibilities. Truth isn't." If you want to understand the deepest sources of power in the modern world, you need to understand how the custodians of the power of money operate. They are drawn from a small number of family bloodlines, both in the West and East. They involve a complex mix of both great good and true evil;

the story is not a simple one. The wicked ones even have a doctrinal system you've not heard of — *Luciferianism*.

What I would like to suggest to you is that we are now at the very end of a 6000+ year cycle of this phenomenon, originating in Babylon (and its collapse) and tracing through the Silk Road and Roman Empire and beyond. There is no precedent to draw upon in our written history or personal experience for what is unfolding now.

The power of fiat money and central banks has led all of humanity to the brink of total disaster. We cannot socially or ecologically sustain another world war. Civil society is at a breaking point, as we've "monetized" all social care (like that for infants and the elderly). Yet there is never enough money... by design, leading to neglect and the breakdown of core institutions like the nuclear family.

The unacknowledged reality is that there is a spiritual war raging around us, and it can be seen in classical terms of light versus dark. The good news is that the light is winning, as it always eventually must. For, however you describe and define it, the universe fundamentally is interconnected and seeks unity. Evil always collapses under its conceit that it can maintain separateness. It is like a physics of morality: it takes non-linear energy to compartmentalize us and resist the unifying power of love.

What is happening right now — and yes, this will appear to be phantasmagorical to many — is the final unfolding of a process and plan that appears to have been hatched over decades (if not centuries). The old central banking system (Bretton Woods onwards) is being replaced — globally — with a new model. Indeed, Iraq is the first country to be "live" in a new financial system of a hard asset-backed currency. No longer will it be possible to fund wars via fiat currency; if you try, you will be cut off from the rest of the global economy.

The Chinese are supplying the gold as collateral, the Americans are ending the corrupt, private Federal Reserve (and preparing to prosecute the banksters and politicians), the BRICS are taking the lead (e.g. the CIPS system that bypasses SWIFT), the gold-backed petroyuan is live, the

Euro is toast (just wait until you hear about the Iran deal's corruption...), and countries like Zimbabwe and Vietnam are experiencing a major revaluation to the new model. It's all out there if you care to look — just because the (Luciferian-controlled) mainstream media isn't telling you doesn't mean it isn't happening.

Over the next few months and years, there is going to be a Great Awakening as society comes to terms with some staggering and unexpected changes. In particular, we will learn about crimes against humanity that have been perpetrated under the old fiat money regime — some well-known, others not so much. The level of embedded corruption (and blackmail, pedophilia and treason) is going to astound most people who are only beginning their journey of awareness.

It took us 6000 years to get into this mess, so fixing it won't be quick or painless. However, just as there is a negative "occult" power in the world that enslaves us, there are also unseen positive forces for good. You've seen the surprise reunification of Korea, and it seems far more is in store, including a historic peace in the Middle East. There has never been a better time to be alive.

Those of us in the tech industry will be challenged to rethink our purpose and products. If double-entry bookkeeping is the original sin of money management, we have to be careful when scaling it with distributed ledgers. Just because there's a number in a computer doesn't mean someone has to be punished by a creditor. Our job is to re-establish social gift economies and reinvent the incentives for a society where money has a different meaning.

In the meantime, give your thanks to those who are in harm's way. This is also a "hot" war against an evil and corrupt system, albeit a silent war still invisible to most of the public. Dismantling human trafficking networks (i.e., slavery and rape) requires confronting the most evil of humanity. Many selfless people are in constant danger, and while we may be impatient for justice and change, the top priority right now is a safe transition.

ᔓ

The Storm: How to Prepare for a Global Corruption Purge

August 21, 2019

IT IS NOT A NOVEL insight to point out that major geopolitical change is an ongoing process. Key events in living memory would include:

» 1970s — oil shock; Vietnam War

» 1980s — deregulation; sudden end of the Soviet empire

» 1990s — Gulf War; dotcom boom and bust

» 2000s — 9/11 + Iraq War; financial collapse

Large-scale change happens

Here in the late 2010s, it is arguable that we are seeing the decline and end of globalism, together with many of its supporting institutions and doctrines. While the countertrend is labeled nationalism by the media, it is better seen as anti-authoritarianism. The demand is for power to be held closer to the people, rather than by an unaccountable political establishment.

Anti-globalism is the narrative that joins together otherwise seemingly disparate events: mass protests in Hong Kong, Brexit in the UK, a "cold" civil war in France, a new government in Brazil, and the Trump administration in the USA. Working people are tired of extreme wealth disparities, declining standards of living, and mass migration causing cultural upheaval.

Most of all, ordinary people demand an end to their exploitation through endemic corruption. Specifically, a two-tier justice system has evolved where a privileged class can easily evade consequences for thieving behavior. This powerful stateless mafia — which controls many important political, financial, media and industrial institutions — now faces removal and justice.

Corruption: The world's biggest industry

We have seen a number of corruption scandals break recently, including:

» Pharma — illegal pushing of addictive opiates to the public

» Banking — LIBOR scandal, US mortgage fraud, 1MDB in Malaysia that may take down Goldman Sachs by the time it's done

» Industrials — huge accounting fraud at GE

» Google — involvement in espionage and treason on behalf of China

» Hollywood — Weinstein is a foretaste of its (child) rape culture being exposed

» Social Media — large-scale rigging of elections

» Catholic Church — cover-up of child abuse

Now that the Mueller investigation has collapsed into nothing of consequence, there are at least six major scandals about to break in Washington DC:

» Pedogate — Epstein Island and the blackmail operations associated with it (NXIVM, SNCTM); UK royal family's involvement plus MI6; Israel and Mossad's dirty role; Hollywood's elite (notably at Disney) are up to their necks in this filth.

» Spygate — Obama personally authorizing illegal FISA spying on the Trump administration, before and after the election. Draws FVEY spy network nations into the scandal, especially Britain.

» Russiagate failed coup attempt — Brennen, Clapper, Comey, Ohr, etc. are all going to hang for treason. Italy has already cleaned house on this one, having been implicated in the set-up.

» Election fraud in 2016 and 2018 by the Democratic party (and for many years before). May trigger the unseating of many in the House and special elections.

- » Clinton Foundation — sale of state secrets to China; Haiti human trafficking (cf. Epstein).
- » Uranium One — illegal sale of US nuclear material to Russia (which draws Mueller into his own scandal…).

Corruption is a widespread phenomenon. Anti-corruption initiatives have a long history. Multinational business has been a thing for centuries. That there *might* be a coordinated, multi-country corruption purge should not be a matter of great controversy.

It is the confluence of so many *simultaneous* major scandals that is what gives #TheStorm its moniker and "black swan" outlier status. It will sweep away some compromised institutions and put many previously untouchable people in jail. This is a paradigm change in government and business, restoring trust and honor that have been missing for decades.

The end of the American "Deep State"

Whether it has been the East India Company, the Venetians, or the Spanish in South America, international trade has always allied to intelligence gathering — and trodden a fine line between legitimate commerce and organized crime (e.g. the opium wars, theft of gold).

To understand #TheStorm we need to recognize that the problem of a two-tier justice system itself comes from transnational crime cartels. Corruption has its own business model, strategies, and organizational design patterns. "Institutionalized crime" syndicates are often of a military-like nature, with power coming from spying, clandestine operations, subversion, esoteric science, and deception.

That power is tied to specific families and secret societies, many being in Europe and Asia. From its founding, the United States has been fighting against fifth columnists, who were often working on behalf of European banking, aristocratic and religious powers. They have used their military intelligence networks to infiltrate American institutions and install their own people — who often become celebrated as quintessentially "American" in the process!

Three notable and well-documented events from the 1940s–1970s paint the contextual picture:

» *Operation Paperclip* imported thousands of key members of the German Nazi regime into important scientific, academic and military posts after WW2.

» *Operation Northwoods* showed the (corrupted) US Government was willing to use "false flag" attacks by its military against its own people for geopolitical ends.

» *Operation Mockingbird* weaponized the US mass media against its own population, using agents who were covertly under the control of the CIA, a rogue intelligence agency under criminal leadership.

An unconstitutional private central bank — the Federal Reserve — was able to print as much money as necessary to bribe whomever it saw fit. This funded the activities of allied crooked banks, media companies and military-industrial corporations. Collectively these "Deep State" actors over time compromised the US judicial, legal and political systems — and subverted the Constitution.

Trump's *de facto* military government

Once civilian institutions are vastly compromised, the only remaining way to peacefully reverse these changes is via the military. Trump is far more than a figurehead, but to focus on him alone is to miss the big picture. He is the most visible part of a multi-decade Patriot plan to retake the country from the bankster criminals and give it back to its people.

The Trump administration explicitly advertises itself as "not just another 4-year election" cycle — *"Our movement is about replacing a failed and corrupt political establishment with a new Government controlled by you, the American people."* It would be wise to take Trump and his generals literally when they state their intentions, as their lives are on the line.

You can see Trump's affinity with the military through his:

» Inauguration — where he unusually and symbolically had soldiers appear behind him.

» Choices of personnel, being surrounded by generals, especially from the Marines.

» Famous "calm before the storm" remark while gathered with his senior military team, with whom he is often pictured on social occasions.

» Focus on celebrating the military and its independence from foreign control for the July 4th celebrations this year.

» Links to Admiral Rogers and General Flynn, who know where the bodies are buried and have been involved in the resulting intrigue.

A deeply embedded crime network has had effective control over the US DOJ, FBI, and CIA — as illustrated by the Clintons' magical escapes from justice. A similar purge of corruption and taming of the Federal Reserve was attempted under JFK; it failed. The protection that the President needs can only come from a loyal military.

The "Q" program of using open-source intelligence to bypass the compromised mass media is further evidence that this is a *de facto* military government with a civilian varnish. The legal and justice systems are being cleaned up, and the "pioneer public" is being primed for stunning revelations that will shake the foundations of society.

#TheStorm is about to make landfall

Sessions, Durham, Huber, Horowitz, Rosenstein, Barr — there are objective reasons to believe that large DOJ legal teams have been quietly working for a considerable period under these leaders. Their task is to indict those responsible for scandals such as those listed previously. Some of these teams have completed their jobs, according to the DOJ website.

There has already been a record-breaking surge of indictments, arrests and convictions for human trafficking. Extensive building work has been done at Guantanamo Bay, and a new senior judge has been appointed for military tribunals there. An enabling executive order on courts martial has been issued, and federal capital punishment has been reinstated. The President has made many proclamations on the treasonous nature of the offences, and he has insisted that they must never recur.

What will happen in late 2019 and early 2020 is that multiple, *connected* scandals are all going to break in fast succession. They will involve crimes against humanity, horrors we had hoped had ended with the Nazis, Chairman Mao, and Pol Pot. A recurring theme from insider leaks is that the trials are going to be televised as a kind of "Nuremberg 2.0."

Trump is not a politician. #TheStorm is not politics. This is about fixing the framework in which politics happen. #TheStorm is a restoration of the American Republic under control of its citizens and the Constitutional rule of law. The conspiracies against the people are very real, and their prosecution is now inevitable.

Who else? What else? Where else?

These events are going to shock most of the public, who have been lulled into complacency by a media conspiracy of silence. They will be scared and confused, since they will not know whom to trust, how bad the situation has been, or whether it is sufficiently contained.

Now is the time that forward-looking leaders can begin to prepare, so you can honestly state that this is on your radar, and you are taking proactive steps to manage the situation. There is ample evidence of this being a very real and serious situation; to ignore it is irresponsible.

We can be reasonably certain that the following will experience major impacts from #TheStorm:

» Political foundations that are used to launder bribes and payoffs (e.g. under the cover of "book deals").

» Charities that are nothing of the kind, being covers for illegal activities.

» NGOs that have a covert purpose (e.g. Red Cross involvement in organ harvesting and human trafficking).

» Multi-national corporations who are using slave labor or have operations in certain politically risky countries (e.g. Apple being forced to repatriate manufacturing from China).

» Financial industry players, with many banks having large fraud liabilities. It is no secret that some, like Bank of America, Citibank, HSBC, Wells Fargo, and Deutsche Bank, face trouble, having indulged in nefarious business practices.

» Media industry, which faces a cataclysmic loss of trust by the public as its past misdeeds and methods get exposed to the light.

» Telecoms and IT, which is the foundation for a great deal of espionage. Amazon is tainted by its CIA associations; Google faces a total brand meltdown.

» Energy, as a great deal of corruption is tied to oil and gas extraction and commodity trading, as well as the push for renewables driven by illegitimate concerns.

#TheStorm will reveal three scams, that are each trillions of dollars in scope, which will further damage the reputation of the media, academia, government, and religious bodies:

» War-for-profit (drawing in banks, arms industry, and public and private intelligence agencies).

» Carbon tax (there is no "climate emergency").

» Fraud through foreign aid.

So what and what next?

This is a "trust apocalypse": those who you were taught were most worthy of trust will repeatedly be proven to have betrayed it. Conversely, you will discover who the truly trustworthy are, as the lies and scams are exposed.

Confronting something of this magnitude in our own lifetimes can seem rather daunting. The MBA strategy books focus mainly on the positive creation of value in the legitimate economy. Where they touch on fraud and crime, value creation comes with tight boundaries in topics like "revenue assurance" and "business continuity planning."

The collapse of a longstanding, massive network of organized crime that intersects with every sector has no precedent. There are no chapters for this kind of scenario in the textbooks. We just know that the November 2020 election cycle is a forcing function: the "swamp" needs to be exposed before then — so that the public will clamor for total drainage.

To deal with this situation, here are some initial suggestions as to how you can take action now:

» **Get your own personal affairs in order as a hygiene factor.** You can't sort other people's problems if your own are a distraction. Clear the decks of anything optional or troublesome.

» **Set your moral compass now.** Those who thrive post-Storm will have different values to those who prospered before it. Be perfectly clear with yourself what you and your organization truly stand for, and what isn't changing, or non-negotiable.

» **Expand your information sources.** The mass media has been compromised by decades of infiltration and corruption. They are complicit in serious crime, if only via a conspiracy of silence, and cannot tell you the whole story. You need to look to alternative sources of journalism and analysis for an accurate picture.

» **Build your human network.** Consider creating a temporary and informal organization to track and make sense of these changes. Use a "who knows, who cares, who can" model to draw in those sufficiently informed, motivated and resourced to act voluntarily and on their own initiative.

» **Limit your exposure.** Manage your risk of exposure to Deep State-aligned companies and sectors. Think about the most important business contracts you have and whether they are robust enough for this kind of outlier business event. Begin to plan contingencies for disruptions on both your supply and demand sides.

» **Map possible opportunities.** This is going to be a one-off opportunity to acquire talent from tainted institutions, buy up businesses at distressed prices, and occupy vacated market roles whose previous holders have been razed by #TheStorm. Making "good enough" moves quickly is likely to beat waiting for perfect certainty. Start making your shopping list.

☙

Crossing the Schism

October 22, 2019

A truth's initial commotion is directly proportional to how deeply the lie was believed. It wasn't the world being round that agitated people, but that the world wasn't flat. When a well-packaged web of lies has been sold gradually to the masses over generations, the truth will seem utterly preposterous and its speaker a raving lunatic.
— (Perhaps) Donald James

IN 1991, GEOFFREY MOORE PUBLISHED one of the most popular business books of the modern era, *Crossing the Chasm*. He highlighted the difference between visionary early adopters of a new technology and the pragmatic majority, who have more grounded needs. While those of an enthusiast mindset may be willing to endure significant complexities and failures to get the benefit of a product, that is not true of consumers in general. As a result, many products fail to "cross the chasm" of mass adoption.

Evil intent has artificially divided society

If we think of all technologies as being expressions of a core idea, then political ideas are "products" too; they are "marketed" to the public and "adopted" by some voters. A political "hot seller" in the United States right now is Make America Great Again (MAGA). Just look at the attendance numbers for Trump rallies if you have any doubt about its popularity.

MAGA in turn is a "brand" of the Great Awakening multinational movement, that seeks to overturn 2-tier justice and endemic corruption on a global basis. It is no secret that MAGA is a "Marmite" offer — that is to say, like the infamous British spread, which people either love or hate, with little middle ground. This divide is a schism in society, and one which cannot be sustained indefinitely.

My sense is that we are close to the moment when major events, long anticipated, break through into the collective consciousness. The socially engineered chasm of belief, which is not a natural phenomenon, is going to have to be bridged for society to survive and thrive.

A nightmare has been our reality

In the next few weeks many anticipate the Horowitz Report to be (finally!) published as part of an ongoing declassification process. As Inspector General of the Department of Justice, he is expected to reveal horrifying levels of corruption during the Obama administration. This has been covered up by a controlled, complicit, and criminal mass media — which has spun a vast web of deceit.

Whereas the Mueller Report was a nothingburger, this will be the opposite: the Watergate scandal multiplied by a force of one thousand. Huber and Durham are also working on their reports, revealing yet more treason, sedition, murder, trafficking, and (almost incredibly) worse — a coup attempt. The mass media and entertainment industries face an apocalypse, especially as their evil culture is exposed.

The result will be a need for the "late adopters" and "laggards" to "cross the schism," since reality is on the other side. Their illusions about the world will be shattered, painfully so. It will be incumbent upon the rest of us to compassionately help them to realign themselves, however uncomfortable that is for both them and us. For, we are all learning that many of our foundational beliefs about the world are built upon fraudulent claims.

I have recently come across a number of snippets of data that I believe will help those who have been victims of media brainwashing and will assist them in coming to grips with the wickedness wrought upon them. These data points will also be of use to those who have already "crossed the schism" (or were never on the wrong side), providing a "rope bridge" that allows for safe passage over.

Nobody wants to discover mid-life that their mind has been sabotaged and their spirit abused. To gain a foundation for benevolent change we must acknowledge whatever is false as being a deception; we must instead identify with whatever is real. Ultimately this is about a personal growth journey from "dark to light." It involves abandoning (unconscious) fear as our core driver in life and embracing (conscious) joy in its place.

How evil authority usurps identity

As a fugitive from the Jehovah's Witness cult, I am authentically familiar with how good people with fine minds can have their identities subverted and stolen. Lies that have been told over long periods — four generations in my family's case — become so entrenched and embedded in the psyche and social structure that they can be almost impossible to escape.

There is a superb 2005 book that covers this issue, which sadly is very hard to locate in paper form; it is called *The End of All Evil* by Jeremy Locke. Thankfully, anyone can download the PDF version, easily located with a web search. For once I believe vital public interest overrides any copyright issues, so I urge you to spread it around. Here is the quote that I wish to highlight (my emphasis):

> Evil uses the authority principle to condition people to obey without questioning what, why or whom they are obeying. **Destroying your identity to gain power over you is the modus operandi of evil.**

Here is how this plays out in our world. People buy into the evil *illusion of authority* of the mass media. They get the same wrong data from The Pravda Times, Pravda Today, Pravda News Network, Pravda Broadcasting Company, American Pravda, Pravda Street Journal, My Pravda, Pravdacast, Pravdabook, Public Pravda System, Scientific Pravda, Pravdaflix, The Pravda, and National Pravda.

They are all independent news sources doing honest journalism, right? Right? Well, no — they are not! All have been infiltrated and subverted to sell a single message of the incumbent powerful orthodoxy. Just because the *Watchtower* and *Awake!* magazines agree on an issue doesn't mean you've triangulated opinion. These are just facets of one totalitarian system that has hidden itself very successfully — until now.

There is essentially *no* truly independent mass media in the United States at present. The corporate media is in the business of *power and control over you*, **not** *truth to hold power to account*. They achieve this by defining — in an Orwellian sense — what the very nature of truth is. To them, "truth" is whatever *authority tells you it is*. Anyone who rejects their **authority to define reality** — and asserts their sovereign right to think for themselves — is ridiculed and ostracized.

The problem of evil is not a new one

That evil works by assuming authority, and then deceiving people to hijack identity, is not a radical or new proposition. It is as old as any of our documented history. To make the point of its longstanding nature, the Bible — not a reference I typically use in my newsletters — brings this issue up in 2 Timothy 4:3–4, KJV, thus:

> For the time will come when they will not endure sound doctrine; but after their own lusts shall they heap to themselves teachers, having itching ears; And they shall turn away their ears from the truth, and shall be turned unto fables.

That the public gorge themselves on comforting lies, much as they do with junk food, is well known. A quote (mis?)attributed to John Swinton, former Chief of Staff of the New York Times from c. 1880, runs:

> There is no such thing, at this date of the world's history, in America, as an independent press. ...If I allowed my honest opinions to appear in one issue of my paper, before twenty-four hours my occupation would be gone. The business of the journalists is to destroy the truth, to lie outright, to pervert, to vilify, to fawn at the feet of mammon, and to sell his country and his race for his daily bread. You know it and I know it, and what folly is this toasting an independent press? We are the tools and vassals of rich men behind the scenes. We are the jumping jacks;

> they pull the strings and we dance. Our talents, our possibilities and our lives are all the property of other men. We are intellectual prostitutes.

To question the veracity of the mass media in the present is not some radical proposition: it is basic common sense, grounded in overwhelming historical evidence. These failed media institutions are primarily agents of lawless power, not individual liberty.

Evil exploits our base weakness

To understand why the public has such an appetite for falsehood, and how these patterns sustain themselves, we must draw back to the grandest possible sweep of history. It has been said that culture is upstream of politics, and religion is upstream of culture. The subversion of our beliefs over thousands of years has led to practical (and awful) consequences in the present.

A "spiritual lie" can be leveraged into a "cultural deception." This then forms the basis for a "political fraud" — which infects every activity and type of organization as a result. A quote by Delamer Duverus from the opening of Bill Cooper's famous and prescient *Behold a Pale Horse* captures this thought:

One
basic
truth can
be used as
a foundation for
a mountain of lies,
and if we dig down deep
enough in the mountain of lies,
and bring out that truth, to set it
on top of the mountain of lies; the entire
mountain of lies will crumble under the weight of
that one truth, and there is nothing more devastating to a
structure of lies than the revelation of the truth upon which

the structure of lies was built, because the shock waves of the revelation of the truth reverberate, and continue to reverberate throughout the Earth for generations to follow, awakening even those people who had no desire to be awakened to the truth.

So, what might be the "one basic truth" that we have failed to recognize, and which might bring down the "mountain of lies," liberating generations to come? The "big lie" is the idea that we are *less than divine* — that is to say, of **less than infinite intrinsic worth.**

This in turn makes us seek validation by temporal authority in the ordinary world. It is an "identity hole" that we seek to fill via externally supplied spiritual meaning. The absence of that meaning — such as exclusion from the "respectable club" for wrongthink — then becomes a source of overwhelming fear.

Merely the threat of having our source of fake spiritual meaning taken away is a powerful leverage point for social control. That is our core vulnerability, our "information security" weak point, which is then "hacked." Once our spiritual meaning "firmware" is subverted, it doesn't matter what happens at the cultural "operating system" or political "application" levels. We can never be secure in our own identity.

We are in a spiritual war (like it or not)

The battle we presently face is one which seems to have raged throughout human history. Who gets to labor in the fields under a hot sun versus who enjoys the feasting afterwards, gorging themselves on fine wine and nubile bodies? There have always been high rewards for psychopathy and awful costs to slavery.

The harsh discovery is how the problems of modernity — like debt slavery from usury — can be traced back for millennia. We are in a long-term war of attrition and subversion by competing factions, and humanity's present challenges have Babylonian (and earlier) origins. It's a simple by-product of how our deepest (manipulated) beliefs are those which have been around the longest (e.g. the role of money and debt in society).

Without understanding deceptions that come from ancient history, few of the present hoaxes can be fully perceived. American artist Suzy Kassem captures this well from a modern Gen X perspective:

> Most of the time, we see only what we want to see, or what others tell us to see, instead of really investigating to see what is really there. We embrace illusions only because we are presented with the illusion that they are embraced by the majority. When in truth, they only become popular because they are pounded at us by the media with such an intensity and high level of repetition that its mere force disguises lies and truths. And like obedient schoolchildren, we do not question their validity and swallow everything up like medicine. Why? Because since the earliest days of our youth, we have been conditioned to accept that the direction of the herd, and **authority anywhere — is always right**.

The fight between false external *authority* (like the corporate mass media) and the divine right to *decide for ourselves* (as we are self-sovereign) is the essence of this everlasting spiritual war. It is an endless fight against deception, infiltration and subversion that demands obedience. We are always having our spiritual, cultural and political beliefs manipulated by powerful psychopaths. Our identity is hijacked for *their* benefit — and *our* enslavement.

Intellectualism as a serious handicap

That the root issue lies in the spiritual realm creates a massive problem in our modern technological world. The presumption of the liberal, progressive educated class is that their intellectual capability and credentials protect them from such deception. This is the exact opposite of reality.

A friend recently lent me *Propaganda: The Formation of Men's Attitudes*, the classic 1962 book by French philosopher Jacques Ellul, author also of *The Technological Society*. The introduction captures the issue succinctly (my emphasis):

> Ellul follows through by designating intellectuals as virtually the most vulnerable of all to modern propaganda, for three reasons: They absorb the largest amount of second-hand, unverifiable information. They feel a compelling need to have an opinion on every important question of our time, and thus easily succumb to opinions offered to them by propaganda on all such indigestible pieces of information. They consider themselves capable of "judging for themselves." **They literally need propaganda.**

This matches my personal experience. I am prone to believing what I want to hear, but I also happen to presume all offered belief systems are frauds — until proven otherwise — as a side effect of my childhood traumas. The pattern I see repeated over and over among educated and intelligent associates —especially those in the tech industry — is they feel that they are "too clever" to be deceived by emotional manipulation.

In reality, they are the perfect "mark": they have mistaken *intellectual* intelligence for *intuitive* intelligence, and they are absolutely not the same thing. Their need for external meaning — resulting from the internal "divinity deficit" — is the strongest. They are the *most* prone to clutch at manufactured belief systems to fill this unconscious spiritual and emotional void.

Some things really are so stupid that only an intellectual would believe them! It seems in retrospect that the separation of science from divinity, and hence its divorce from *moral* philosophy, was a big mistake.

How to cross the schism — and defeat evil?

In conclusion, I would like to leave you with three thoughts that might help us to collectively "cross the schism" by reaching out to one another over the scary divide.

1. Love thy deluded neighbor

The classic exhortation seems almost trite, but it has a purpose here. People change when they reject a painful status quo, and feel (not think!) that change is to their benefit. Feelings are facts! They can hear the upside of change when it is offered to them in a kind and appreciative manner. If someone feels loved, they will be able to receive the gift of a pathway to positive change.

The cruelty of the social engineering that has been performed via mass media is to make those offering the truth appear to be hateful — "racist, sexist, xenophobic," and so on. This could not be further from reality, but it is what it is. The growth challenge for those who have "crossed the schism" is to send "love letters" backwards, not "hate mail." In a spiritual war zone, lovingness is persuasiveness.

2. Seek unifying synthesis over separating analysis

Recently I offered the following thought on Twitter:

> I can think of many prostitutes, junkies, and queers I know who exhibit kindness, empathy, and generosity — and who will be taking the VIP fast track entry into heavenly realms, while the judgmental, self-righteous, and sanctimonious may be ticketless and excluded outside.

In response I got the following erudite observation (edited):

> To put it another way: God wants us to be compassionate and moral, not compassionate OR moral. Half of humanity justifies immorality by their compassion, the other justifies indifference and hostility by scrupulous moralism. **Dueling hypocrisies.**

The analytical mind sees the dualism of "two sides," and attempts to pick the "best" one. The synthesist, on the other hand, works to reconcile the difference. Beware falling into the trap of "dueling hypocrisies."

3. Create beauty: it is a universal language

For myself, I have taken up photography as a means of rebalancing my intellectual intelligence with my intuitive side. It has done me unbounded good, helping me to appreciate the ordinary, feel gratitude for any place, and experience more of the joy of being alive. It is indeed a divine activity, reconnecting myself to the world around me in a "present in the moment" and sensual manner.

The works I have produced are — I am told — often beautiful, and I share them at the end of every newsletter for a purpose. It is not just to show off my talent! Rather, it is to offer the one thing that we can agree on: that the world around us, that we all share regardless of contradictory belief, is a beautiful one. Even if my words repel someone, they know I am human.

For, we humans are all divine — of infinite worth! We can naturally reconnect to one another via our innate and shared sense of beauty. Spiritually grounded art is a tool that helps us to cross the (temporary) cultural and political schism that separates us.

#WWG1WGA

The ideal tyranny is that which is ignorantly
self-administered by its victims.
The most perfect slaves are, therefore,
those which blissfully and
unawaredly enslave themselves.
— (also perhaps) Donald James

ᔕ

Dark and Light: The Revolution Within

November 24, 2019

If an egg is broken by outside force, life ends.
If broken by inside force, life begins.
Great things always begin from inside.
— Jim Kwik

AS I GET OLDER and life's dramas unfold, it becomes more apparent that others may have left behind some wisdom worth paying attention to. We are all individually special, yet every aspect of our experience is ordinary in some way since the basic patterns of being human never change. I'd like to share a few of the wiser words that I have recently collected.

As context, I spent 30+ years being rewarded for developing "intellectual intelligence." The human mind models the outside world, and the focus of our attention then becomes located in the head. In computer science terms, we have a "model, view, controller" paradigm, and "mind models" give us the power of *control* over the outer world that we view through our senses.

There are some problems with this approach to life. From a personal perspective, it leaves us as "hominid crabs" with one vastly overdeveloped "head limb," and one pathetic trailing stump of a "heart limb." We can easily be manipulated via emotions and sensory stimuli, yet wrongly believe our intellect protects us from propaganda. From a societal outlook, "control" is the mindset of the psychopath, tempting us away from a loving, heart-centered paradigm. This seduces us into consenting to "pathocracy," becoming a cog in a political and economic machine that strip mines our humanity.

In the past few years I have worked hard to rebalance myself to be less "crabby." A series of unplanned events led me to reconnect with my "intuitive intelligence," notably through photographic art. My newsletter subscribers may have noticed that I include one of my efforts at the end of every newsletter, so that the clever wordsmith gets paired with the caring pixel painter. It is meant to also encourage others to give art a try since all humans are born artists.

I have also had to do plenty of "inner work" over the past decade, which is reflected in what I create and write today. I summarized my learning from this experience recently in a tweet:

> Intellectual intelligence seeks the feeling of knowing.
> Intuitive intelligence seeks the knowing of feeling.

The two kinds of intelligence feed into each other, as a kind of "figure eight." What matters is their integration, not their separation. This brought the following insightful response:

> Intellect is a way of knowing that sources from thinking.
> Intuition is a way of knowing that sources from feeling.
> Both intellect and intuition are core forms of human intelligence.
> Balance is the key.

This sense of mind vs body knowledge is embedded into folklore as "know thyself" or "you are only as sick as your secrets." An awareness that is only located in the head, and ignores the heart, is unhealthy. Albert Einstein said it thus:

> The intuitive mind is the sacred gift, and the rational mind
> is the faithful servant. We've created a world that honors the
> servant and has forgotten the gift.

My dear Christian friends constantly remind me the Bible is chock full of wise words about all kinds of subjects, and this one is no exception. Take 1 Cor 11:31, NKJV: "For if we would judge ourselves, we would not be judged."

My take on this is that the essence of wise action is to combine these two forms of intelligence. We are judged for unwise acts in the world because we have failed to integrate our intuitive and intellectual skills. Likewise, 2 Cor 4:18, KJV:

> We [are to] look not at the things which are seen, but at the things which are not seen: for the things which are seen are temporal; but the things which are not seen are eternal.

This opposes the dogma of scientific materialism, which renders the scientist into a temporary collection of particles, indistinguishable from the outer world — beyond having a skin to separate us. It instead suggests our divine inner conscious essence; the heart observer — when all is quiet in the mind — is eternal and *beyond the material.* I remain an ignostic (distinct from agnostic) on all matters of metaphysics, at least in public!

Carl Jung said, "The hardest thing a man can do is to accept himself fully." That applies here: to deny one's feelings is a common defense against the occasional harshness and cruelty of life. These ideas are not unique to Judeo-Christian societies either, as a meme from my Twitter feed suggests. The meme depicts a quote as originating from Sri Ramana Maharshi (Talk 219): "The only useful purpose of the present birth is to turn within and realize the Self. There is nothing else to do."

The ascendancy of intellectual intelligence over intuitive intelligence is dangerous. Many perceive that we exist in a quasi-totalitarian, transhumanist technocracy. Systems of technological control are overwhelming human empathy. The risks are highlighted in Bill Cooper's classic *Behold a Pale Horse* (which accurately predicted the events of 9/11/2001), where he introduces the idea of technological "silent weapons" that exploit our "disintegrative" weaknesses:

> The public cannot comprehend this [silent] weapon [of control], and therefore cannot believe that they are being attacked and subdued by a weapon. The public rightly instinctively feel that something is wrong, but because of the technical nature of the silent weapon, they cannot express their feeling in a rational way, or handle the problem with intelligence. Therefore, they do not know how to cry for help, and do not know how to associate with others to defend themselves against it.

When we have low intuitive intelligence compared to our intellectual prowess, we have an "attack surface" that the wicked can and do exploit. The result is the ultimate form of betrayal: self-enslavement.

I have watched this unfold for decades, with family members trapped in a cult that stunts spiritual growth (i.e., the integration of intellectual and intuitive intelligence). Its basis of control is a series of both conceptual and emotional lies that its victims accept as truth. The key one is that we are of less than infinite worth, with cult membership "solving" the fear of "eternal nothingness" upon death.

Evil offers us endless doctrines, schemes and temptations to make up our "divinity gap." All are based on our believing lies about our true divine (i.e., infinitely worthy) nature. Russian author Dostoevsky summarizes the danger of lack of intuitive intelligence perfectly in The Brothers Karamazov (my emphasis):

> Above all, don't lie to yourself. The man who lies to himself and listens to his own lie comes to a point that he cannot distinguish the truth **within** him, or **around** him, and so loses all respect for himself and for others. And having no respect he ceases to love.

Accepting a lie is often the result of a failure to recognize the difference between "rational knowing" (i.e., intellect) from the "feeling of knowing" (i.e., intuition). Thoughts and feelings become confused and entwined, allowing fear to displace thought. For, love is the antithesis of fear, and one of my Twitter followers perceptively summarizes the trap we face:

> To embrace the truth is to first realize the folly of the coexistence of fear and logic. Those two cannot coexist together because fear is an illogical destructive force that taints everything it touches.

Thus, to develop sanely and safely as an *intellectual*, one **must** also engage in a **spiritual** path that co-develops *intuitive* understanding. The essence of the **mind control** of the mass media is to **sell us fear** — "the end of the world is coming!" — shutting down our logical processing center.

Trauma displaces thought. The "awakening" process is to paradoxically fully identify with our fears and traumas, so that we may transcend them and think clearly. As another perspicacious follower notes:

> Awakening is a deeply personal inward journey that is largely unique to the one experiencing it. The sooner we learn to trust our own process and the truth we find within, the sooner we can let go of the need for external validation. That's where peace and power align with love.

Everyone has a different set of fears and traumas to integrate, so no two "awakenings" are the same. The darkness doesn't go away, but instead becomes a bearable complement to the light. The end game is an acceptance of **all** that there is, both light **and** dark, intellectual **and** intuitive, transient **and** eternal.

Humanity has been in traumatic darkness for a long time and is presently experiencing more healing light — our collective "dark *to* light." Nonetheless we inhabit a "dark and light" cosmos, with the dark (evil) being a necessary complement of the light (good). The wise will recognize this symbiosis of dark and light, not their opposition.

For a brilliant summary of this profound insight, I recommend a ten-minute video featuring the philosopher Alan Watts. You can find it on Omid Pakbin's YouTube channel or by searching for the title, "Alan Watts Explains What Awakening Means."

∽

The Silent War and Digital Soldiers

February 27, 2020

Men are so simple and so much inclined to obey immediate needs that a deceiver will never lack victims for his deceptions.
— Niccolò Machiavelli

ONE OF THE MOST POWERFUL things one can do is to name a previously unnamed phenomenon. The conflict we are currently immersed in seems to be picking up the moniker *The Silent War.*

Its occult nature is that Silent War happens in the shadows, under the ground, in secret, in the skies, and beyond perception. Just as the Cold War was "like industrialized war, but visibly fought everywhere between nations," this Silent War is "like ye olde war, but invisibly fought everywhere and by everyone."

To make sense of what seems to be going on, I have some data points that may be of help to you. In "How We Stay Blind to the Story of Power," the British investigative journalist Jonathan Cook writes (with my emphasis):

> Very obviously **power's main concern is the ability to conceal itself.** Its exposure as power weakens it, by definition. Once exposed, power faces questions about its legitimacy, its methods, its purposes. Power does not want to be seen, it does not want to be confined, it does not want to be held accountable. It wants **absolute freedom to reproduce itself, and ideally to amass more power.**

Here he hints at the potential for (unaccountable) "dark power" to create systems to reproduce itself as a kind of parasite on the (accountable) "light power" of civil society. Where might this take us? He continues:

> That is why true power makes itself as invisible and as inscrutable as it can. Like a mushroom, power can grow only in darkness.

> That is why it is the hardest thing to write about in ways that are intelligible to those under its spell, which is most of us, most of the time. Because power co-opts language, words are inadequate to the task of describing the story of real power.

Note that this is from someone who identifies with the political left. Power that comes from secrecy and deceit is on a good-evil axis, not left-right. Invisible dark power entraps people, usurps their free will, and appropriates their resources — so as to fuel its evil ends. These in turn are presented as being meritorious and virtuous to its victims!

Carrying this theme further, in "The Origins of the Deep State in North America," Canadian journalist Matthew Ehret writes (again my emphasis):

> If a society can be kept under the control of their belief in what their senses tell them, then the invisible structures governing their behavior will remain mystical and unknowable. More importantly than that, those **intentions shaping such structures towards a pre-determined goal will also remain unknowable.** If unknowable, then beyond the reach of judgement, and if beyond the reach of judgement, then **unchangeable.**

This suggests that such "dark power" might be sustained over very long periods, and with specific goals in mind. How long? Well...

> This has been the great secret of empire since the days of the Babylonian priesthood and Babylon's whore Rome, since whose collapse, three more incarnations have manifested themselves in the forms of the Byzantine, Venice and Anglo-Dutch empires. *This is the dynamic at the heart of what has today come to be known as "the Deep State."*

There is a simplistic view of society that "dark power" is confined to small-scale "conspiracies," and that these cannot coalesce and become a cancer of criminal culture. Exposure would be too easy: one whistleblower, and the media would pick up on it. The existence of totalitarian societies shows this to be false: dark power can grow to displace the light, via violence, subversion and deception.

In the case of the modern West, what if the mass media was itself corrupt to the core, and little more than a mouthpiece for globalist gangster government? What if an alliance of secret societies, intelligence agencies, bloodline families, corrupt officials, and usurious bankers colluded to rob the rest of the population and enslave them? What if they used extortion, blackmail and mind control technology to achieve their ends?

The false assumption of many is that such a totalitarian "Deep State" couldn't happen. An "incredulity barrier" stops otherwise rational people from seeing what is staring them in the face. The Western mass media has sold them endless false flag attacks, fake health scares and fraudulent politicians. Nonetheless, the masses keep on watching the TV news, as if it were healthy and wholesome factual information.

This is captured neatly by the indomitable Joe M, aka @StormIsUponUs, who posted on Twitter on February 25, 2020:

> You know why they stay asleep? Because all those cameras, clean-cut anchors, Ivy League educations, graphics, resources, high-rise buildings, decades of being in my living room — it's IMPOSSIBLE that they could be controlled by a criminal super-mafia trying to destroy the world.

The battle in which we are immersed is one to awaken the masses to a very unpleasant reality. Crimes against humanity have been occurring on our watch, and without us paying attention. Millions of children are disappearing into human trafficking networks, never to be seen again. Billions of people are being poisoned by their food, environment and medicines. Everyone is being ripped off by a banking system founded upon debt slavery, asset bubbles and warmongering. The corporate media is just a mouthpiece of this structural elite.

So, what if the "good people" organized themselves — likely over a long period — to change this tragic and longstanding state of affairs? What if there was an exigency to this process, as the cancer of corruption threatened to kill its host? What if we are right now witnessing The Silent War break through into the open?

The following anonymous post from the boards (that I have truncated) comes via @M2Madness on Twitter:

> If all was revealed it would crash society. Our economy, our people... just because YOU can handle it doesn't mean EVERYONE can. It would put us in wars, it would create havoc across the globe. The reason it's a silent war is because they want to continue with society when it's done.

The Silent War has a traditional kinetic component. For instance, there have been many seismic events that would indicate the destruction of underground military bases, for their signature is not a natural one. There is also a spiritual component, as the Satanic method is to invert right and wrong, and to encourage good people to join in movements with bad outcomes by persuading them (by deception) it is the moral thing to do.

Lastly, and perhaps most importantly, it is an information war. The mass media has been weaponized by criminals — many of whom are loyal to foreign states. This means these institutions literally are enemies of the people. The "guns" of information warfare in the hands of citizens are computers, internet connections and social media. This fight for narrative supremacy — between the Deep State media and the Patriot public — is now coming to a head.

Which is where "digital soldiers" come in — to borrow a term from General Flynn. We are an irregular insurgent force on a real battlefield, with physical world consequences to our fight. This very book is a piece of terrain in the war: I have chosen to speak my mind and to fight. I am a strategic communications asset, too, likely monitored by the military as a consequence. *Glad to be of service!*

Some of us have seen the enemy's eyes, and **we will not cease our pursuit until their propaganda factory is out of action**. No more will we tolerate media being a tool to protect the guilty and ruin the innocent. The days of naively allowing our family to be socially engineered via purported "entertainment" are over.

The mass media's control over the public psyche is dependent on the true nature of "dark power" remaining concealed. Crucial to the mass media's grand deception is that the "dots" — of wars, crimes, and crooks — do not get connected. The public's attention is endlessly drawn from one manufactured story to the next, without them ever being linked. There has, until now, always been a new distraction lined up, ready to seize the headlines should anything awkward come to light that needs to be buried.

As digital soldiers, our battle is to connect what was not connected, to set upright that which was inverted, and to shine light on that power that was previously in the dark. We provide a true, transparent and accountable alternative to the corrupt corporate mass media. This conflict will be won when the masses get the "big picture" of dark power — and how it has abused, robbed and enslaved them for generations.

Expect a noisy Great Awakening to end the Silent War.

Death of a Supermafia

March 25, 2020

If you know the enemy and know yourself,
you need not fear the results of a hundred battles.
— Sun Tzu

WE ARE IN THE FINAL THROES of a war against a supermafia that has plagued humanity for longer than we have records. This "Deep State" criminal network is a form of nationless dark power that has sickened all societies worldwide. It is like an unseen fungus or cancer in the intestines of human culture; it gorges itself on our energy for its own malignant ends.

To understand the Silent War (and present-day events) demands making sense of the invisible enemy we are fighting. The exposure of this supermafia is not a symptom of a global collapse into chaos. Rather, the sighting of the true enemy of humanity is cause for celebration, for it is a precondition of victory.

Here are some pointers that I have picked up from my research over the last few years. They should give you a sense of the shape and methods of this supermafia. Take them as being provisional: I am not an all-knowing sage, and I have no "insider" or privileged knowledge. Just a guy with a laptop — and lots of curiosity.

Hive structure scales well

In my previous incarnation as a telecoms expert, I wrote about Recursive Internet Architecture (RINA). RINA outperforms the design of the current internet — TCP/IP — in every dimension, except one: TCP/IP is deployed everywhere already, which makes RINA adoption "unthinkable."

The Deep State has a *Hivite* culture, which is a bit like RINA. It is "cellular" (a hive) and "recursively layered" (a pyramid), and hence it scales well and "fails well." This is unsurprising — cybernetics tells us this needs to be so via Viable System Theory. This also explains why the focus on "conspiracy theories" is a distraction, because what matters are architectures of criminal cultures.

As with RINA, the Deep State's "recursive" method of operations are "unthinkable" to those who have only experienced the mass media "flat" information monoculture. It is like explaining blockchain applications to someone whose only experience of computing is punched cards. There is a mismatch of the levels of architectural sophistication.

Antifragile doctrines for longevity

The Deep State supermafia has its own religion — the Cult of Osiris — with doctrines that have helped it endure. (The "Lindy effect" is a kind of "theory of evolution" for cultural memes and their longevity.) A critical doctrine is "revelation of the method," which means telling your victim what you plan to do to them beforehand.

This is seen in their psychopathic morality as a means of getting "malinformed consent." That it is not fully informed is deemed the victim's problem. From the perspective of the perpetrator, they were given fair warning, so they have no reason to wriggle out of whatever deal with the devil was on offer.

More deeply, if the victim *does* react, you have a "stressor" to your system that allows you to learn how to adjust to stay unseen. Just as airline safety paradoxically improves with every crash because their causes are always investigated, "covert power" gains ever more "safety from discovery via enhanced stealth" from every failure of "revelation of the method."

This is an *antifragile* scaling property which has allowed their parasitic culture to persist over millennia.

Mutually assured destruction via blackmail

To gain access to this supermafia — whose tentacles run through endless familiar and trusted institutions — you need to pass the "entrance exam." This involves disclosing your darkest secrets and doing illegal acts that bind you to their system of crime. The arrival of photography and videography has turbocharged these blackmail networks in the last century.

Places like Epstein Island are blackmail centers. Pedophilia is a "basic level" activity to gain kompromat. (This is a Russian term for compromising information used for control, extensively practiced by the Soviets.) As you seek access to higher levels of criminal power, you have to perform more depraved acts. There are images I don't want to be responsible for putting in your head. The time will come for the public to know, and there will be a managed process of disclosure.

The consequence of this blackmail is that everyone "in the club" knows that everyone else is blackmailed. In the same way that a VISA or Mastercard logo on a retailer window is a "trustmark" for a legitimate commerce network, they have a "reverse trustmark" for a global crime network.

You can socially signal your insider status — handshakes, clothing, jewelry for example — and you are given access to its illegitimate power.

Addiction via vampirism and cannibalism

Take this next one lightly for now.

It seems that humanity has an intensely dark secret that is seeping out — one that I had previously dismissed as likely disinformation but is becoming too hard to ignore. It appears that the human pineal gland contains a substance produced when under stress — adrenochrome — that is a euphoric and hallucinogenic elixir of youth. The unwanted side effects are fewer or less pernicious when the source is a child rather than an adult.

The stories of vampires were not fictional tales: they are "revelation of the method" of a *pedovore*, cannibal culture. The evidence that has swayed me includes the "rabbit" structure of the adrenochrome molecule and endless "white rabbit," blood sacrifice, and adrenochrome references in both "dark" culture (pop music, art, movies, tech) and "light" (US military, Q, Trump).

The "walnut" of the pineal gland also has multitudinous references in ancient culture and current affairs. At the very least, the access to and drinking of the blood of children appears to be core to their culture. Jimmy Savile wasn't just a child pimp and pedophile, but a necrophiliac too. He wasn't an exception, but rather was a welcomed member of this Satanic ruling class.

The evil involved in farming blood products from young humans is beyond your worst nightmare. It also means that the Satanic culture binds people to it via a lethal addiction. Once you are hooked on adrenochrome, there is no way out, and only one supplier. You are a slave to their drug of death; hence you are completely loyal for life.

Again, take this lightly for now. It's a tentative report and I encourage you to do your own research.

Hoarding of knowledge

Esoteric science is uncontroversially a "thing." There is plenty of knowledge locked up in "black projects" by the military, for example. The question you should be asking yourself, therefore, is what the balance is between exoteric knowledge (available to all) and esoteric (for select insiders only).

It appears that this supermafia has succeeded in "privatizing" much of the "raw data" of society (e.g. via corrupt medical and tech institutions). Meanwhile, they have polluted, erased, and inverted the open and public science and historical record. As some have said, if you think "fake news" is bad, wait until you learn about "fake history" and "fake science."

Once you have eradicated the memory of past events — and possibly even past civilizations and cycles of nature — then you have an almost inconceivable level of power over the public. You can fabricate all kinds of tales of origin and purpose — political, cultural, and even biological — for your own nefarious ends.

The old "successful" brands of "adopted falsehoods" can be leveraged to sell "new models" of false narrative. The labyrinth of lies grows over time and gets harder to escape — at least until the internet arrives bringing us "knowledge ladders" to climb over its "walls of misdirection."

Control over popular culture

To maintain dominance over the "herd of human sheep" — and harvest them for slavery and slaughter — you need only subvert a few beliefs. For instance, if you can persuade the masses that the heads of the supermafia are not crooks, but are kings with a divine right to rule, then you have permanently institutionalized your criminality.

By owning a few "critical nodes" of cultural belief — especially religion and news media — you can maintain effective control over the rest of society. Some basic "information warfare" technologies — like false idols, or divide and conquer identity politics — keep the public busy fighting ghosts and each other, and never identifying the real power.

The political system then becomes a puppet show, with blackmailed actors and "rhetoric robots" entrancing the masses into a contained conflict that only ever serves the criminal structural elite. Their underlying "dark secret" — the blackmail and pedophilia "glue" that binds them all — has been successfully suppressed (until now).

Debt slavery from monetary control

Imagine for a moment you are an Egyptian pharaoh, and you have your slave workforce doing your personal bidding. Having passed your Masters in Bondage Administration, you understand that the laws of economics also apply to slave economies. Supply and demand still matter and have to be balanced. So you issue a scrip (substitute) currency for your slaves to spend at the "company stores" in your "vassal economy."

You notice how some slaves really struggle in times of strife. So you make them a deal: you will loan them extra scrip (at interest) to "tide them over." In return they promise to put in extra labor for you, surrendering their little, remaining leisure. Over time, you find that you can get more and more labor by inducing strife, causing more distress, and making more loans….

You can see where this is going. Usury, taxes, war. The core of our financial system is corrupt and broken. In particular, central banking is the power base of the supermafia. "That's a lovely country you have there, and it would be a terrible shame if it got disconnected from the global financial system." They are called "banksters" for a good reason.

This is why we now need a reboot of our financial system on a new central banking platform, new asset-backed currencies, and the removal of the "pharaoh" supermafia ruling class from running it.

Hijack of trusted institutions into the "family"

It is the most contradictory observation: the supermafia is into child abuse (including of their own), and yet family is the most important thing to them. Let me explain.

The success of the supermafia is through a classic "silver or lead" threat to those in or near "apex" leadership positions. Either you join in and become very rich, or you are killed. Those who join in are adopted into a cross-institutional, mutual self-promotion club. Many of the cultural, political, religious and business leaders you have been taught to admire are controlled members.

Those on the "inside" are "family" — it's not unlike the Sicilian Mafia and the omertà vow of silence. What turns the "mafia" into a "supermafia" is how they:

1. Perpetuate their violence through abuse of their own children for multi-generational "sustainability" of psychopathy. This is the "vertical" scaling over time.
2. Co-opt trusted institutions beyond the traditional "narcotics, prostitution and gambling." This is the "horizontal" scaling to encompass ever more of society.

Many famous multinational corporations are "family businesses" of this supermafia. The scale of the corruption is beyond what most people can presently imagine.

Parasites on the public

Cats can carry a protozoan parasite — Toxoplasma gondii — that causes behavioral changes in other species. For mice, this is a lethal condition, for it causes them to cease fearing cats. There is evidence that many humans — a third of us carry the parasite — also behave erratically as a result.

The supermafia we are dealing with — who are ruthlessly evil — have perfected psychological and spiritual warfare over very long periods. They have learned to weaponize the compassion, kindness and caring of humans, and misuse these for their own ends. What toxoplasmosis does for mice, they have done to humans via a mix of technological, environmental and cultural means.

This is not an abstract matter for me, having seen members of my own family lured into a cult manufactured by this supermafia. They believe they are in service to the highest rodent purpose in life, when they have been deceived into misdirecting their worshipful energy towards the enemy: felines, if you will. An example at the societal level is the "Climate Emergency" carbon tax scam, which preys on otherwise understandable ecological concerns.

The "technocracy" and its amoral, transhumanist agenda is very seductive. None of us are going to come away "clean" from this. We all have colluded and contributed to some degree to our fate, ignoring warning signs that our conveniences and pleasures were unwise or unethical. Those who sit in judgement of the folly of others should be gifted a mirror at the first opportunity.

Pure evil and unlimited violence

Lastly, but most importantly, to make sense of the Deep State supermafia, you need to understand one key thing. It is evil. To the core. That means it has no boundaries on the wickedness it will engage in. Literally none.

I thought industrial scale torture, murder and even cannibalism of children was the worst of it. I was wrong. You need to be thinking of depopulation, genocide and total enslavement. You need to be thinking of deliberately engineered suffering, conflict and death. You need to be thinking of eugenics, human sacrifice and ecocide.

Profiteering from these has been considered mandatory.

And now it is all coming to an end.

#TheStorm

☙

Coronagate: The Scandal to End All Scandals

May 4, 2020

I WAS GOING TO TITLE this chapter "Hydroxychloroquine: Does It Cure CONS" — with the joke being CONS as an abbreviation for Credulous Official Narrative Syndrome. But people dying and losing their livelihoods worldwide for no good reason is not a joke. Coronagate is the political con job that promises to eclipse all others, even against stiff competition like Spygate.

Here's the bottom line: Dr. Fauci and his institutional sponsors have known since at least 2005 that chloroquine — and its milder derivative hydroxychloroquine (HCQ) — inhibit coronaviruses like SARS from replicating in the body. They have withheld this important information from the public and failed to act on it when forming policy. Instead these besuited criminals have pushed experimental and expensive drugs while having huge financial conflicts of interest.

This means that the present lockdown and the immense disruption and harm it is causing is for no real benefit. We could be offering cheap and effective prophylactic and therapeutic treatments for COVID-19, targeted at the vulnerable (like healthcare workers, elderly, those with comorbidities). Indeed, several countries are taking this course now **with proven success**.

Major Western nations are committing economic and social suicide to sustain an enormous lie about the integrity of those we trusted to protect us. This is a crime against humanity and encompasses many in the pharma business, in the corporate media, and in the government. The size of the scandal cannot be overstated. Those responsible deserve the most severe punishment for ruining civil society.

The scammers buy influence over health policy

The Bill and Melinda Gates Foundation has come under intense scrutiny in recent weeks. This entity has "donated":

» At least $200m to the Clinton Foundation, which cannot pass the most rudimentary tests of compliance with charity law; but who could possibly have known it is corrupt.

» Another $250m to WHO, CDC and NIH, who set and approve global health policy, while simultaneously profiting from development and licensing of vaccines in particular.

» Tens of millions of dollars to media companies like NPR, The Guardian, and the BBC, to ensure the media was bought off.

It is "donated" in quotes, as the Foundation has major shareholdings in many pharmaceutical companies and creates personal benefit for Mr. Gates. This is not philanthropy; it is business fraudulently operating under a tax-free regime. Dr. Fauci has sat on his vaccine initiative leadership council — which means he is not a neutral player when it comes to selecting the best treatment on behalf of the public.

George Soros, the Bill and Melinda Gates Foundation, and the WHO are all shareholders in UNITAID, the patent-sharing subsidiary of Gilead, which coincidentally (!) is in Wuhan. Both Gilead and UNITAID have donated to the (ultra-corrupt) Clinton Foundation.

Remdesivir: a false hope

The media has been hyping this drug from Gilead, but you could easily draw the wrong conclusion without knowing the rest of the story:

» The drug is essentially useless as the damage is already done by a virus by the time the drug takes effect.

» The goalposts of the clinical effectiveness study were moved once it became clear that there was no benefit in mortality, only time to recovery.

» There is no statistical significance to even these results.

- There is no evidence that the intended effect (reduction in viral load) actually exists, or actually is timed after the cause (giving the medication).

The conflict of interest between the health policymakers and the salesmen of expensive drugs could not be starker than in this case. The US media knows who pays the piper and thus calls the tune of their editorial. Only the "alt media" is giving anything like the full picture.

A vaccine? Forget it (for now)!

Many are hoping for a vaccine to cure COVID-19, but this is a remote prospect, despite many being under development. First, the virus is mutating and lacks a stable genetic base. We don't even have tests at this point with reliable false positive/negative rates since we don't know the mutation rate and profile.

Second, there is a massive scandal of the vaccine industry claiming to have quality controls when it lacked them. This lie now appears to have enabled all kinds of foreign DNA and viruses to enter humans, with mouse viruses potentially having caused an epidemic of human cancer. This is not the first time, for SV40 monkey viruses having contaminated polio vaccines to the same effect. Public trust is deservedly low, and you cannot claim legal immunity from negligence.

Finally, the RNA technologies being proposed are novel and have no safety case. Their testing on humans without animal studies first is likely criminal. Establishing their effectiveness and long-term safety will take many years. Given the understandable lack of public trust, getting them adopted voluntarily will be an uphill struggle. Doing it coercively involves breaches of human rights and the Hippocratic oath.

This means we need to look elsewhere for treatments.

Hydroxychloroquine: the evidence of its effectiveness

The most compelling data for HCQ comes from Italy. Sixty-five thousand patients using it long-term for other conditions resulted in 20 COVID-19 infections and zero deaths. Turkey has made it the standard protocol for treatment of all COVID-19 patients, and has a low death rate as a result. Indeed, a whole list of nations, including India, have followed this path and are giving it prophylactically to healthcare workers too. Israel has secured supplies of HCQ at the head-of-state level, and the Israelis are notoriously not stupid when it comes to medicine. Israel is allowing doctors to run their own trials with HCQ and has a very low death rate.

The Association of American Physicians and Surgeons has endorsed the use of HCQ as being 90% effective, noting:

> To date, the total number of reported patients treated with HCQ, with or without zinc and the widely used antibiotic azithromycin, is 2,333, writes AAPS, in observational data from China, France, South Korea, Algeria, and the U.S. Of these, 2,137 or 91.6 percent improved clinically. There were 63 deaths, all but 11 in a single retrospective report from the Veterans Administration where the patients were severely ill.

There are successful studies on HCQ in the USA — 95% reduction in death; France — 88% reduction in death; and Brazil — 95% reduction in death. The only unsuccessful one was in the USA at the Veterans Administration; it was manifestly rigged to produce its result by retrospective selection of an adverse population and giving the wrong protocol at the wrong time.

While we might wish to have a double-blind, randomized, controlled trial, we don't have the time to perform one. Too many people will die unnecessarily. We understand the mechanism by which HCQ operates (opening the cell to allow zinc as the standard antiviral to enter) and when and how to give it (as early in infection as possible, together with antibiotics to protect the lungs).

The "plandemic panic"

The British justification for lockdown and abandonment of "herd immunity" comes from the work of Prof. Neil Ferguson of Imperial College in London. This institution has received over $185m from the Gates

Foundation. He has a truly appalling track record, having grotesquely mis-modelled foot and mouth disease, Creutzfeldt-Jakob disease, H5N1, and swine flu. But he was hired again for COVID-19, where he was only out by a factor of 20 on mortality, and made obvious errors like presuming frail elderly patients would need ventilators when this is well known to be inadvisable (as it kills them).

The combination of a cataclysmic death forecast with no known treatment is what then drove draconian lockdown policy. This was despite the policy being implemented so late it cannot have had any impact on the actual peak demand for healthcare. Whether done with integrity or as sabotage only history can tell. The damage is done now.

It is not just the UK where statistics have been used to terrorize the public into submission. In Italy, a member of parliament — Vittorio Sgarbi — made a statement to:

> [denounce] the closure of 60% of the businesses for 25,000 COVID-19 Deaths, of which the National Institute of Health says 96.3% died NOT of COVID-19 but of other pathologies. That means only 925 have died of the virus. 24,075 have died of other things.

The crime

The smoking gun is a Virology Journal paper from the NIH (2005), where Dr. Fauci was director: **"Chloroquine is a potent inhibitor of SARS coronavirus infection and spread."** COVID-19 is a SARS virus similar to the one discussed in 2005. It is undeniable that this information was public and known to Dr. Fauci and his colleagues.

The immediate consequence has been a massive misallocation of resources — Nightingale hospitals in London and other UK cities have been empty. Our healthcare system has failed to deliver care to many needing urgent operations for other illnesses.

The death toll from COVID-19 increasingly looks small compared to those from lockdown. There are an estimated 18,000 excess dead from cancer in the UK (due to delayed diagnosis and treatment) — up to 150,000 dead in UK from lockdown. If translated to the US by population, that could be three-quarters of a million people dead from lockdown by the time this is all over. I hope the numbers come in far below this, but the negative health consequences of isolation and poverty are well known.

We also now face a massive loss of liberties and imposition of de facto martial law. This last point is not a minor one. Lord Sumption — a member of the British Supreme Court — writes in the Daily Mail:

> To say that life is priceless and nothing else counts is just empty rhetoric. People say it because it is emotionally comfortable and avoids awkward dilemmas. But they don't actually believe it.
>
> We went to war in 1939 because lives were worth losing for liberty. We allow cars on the roads because lives are worth losing for convenience. We travel by air although pollution kills. We tut-tut about it, but we willingly do it.

To claim that all that matters is COVID-19 deaths is to insult all those with other mortal conditions, ignore those who will die from lockdown itself, and invalidate other valid goals like liberty. It is a narcissistic and masochistic position: "Look how virtuous I am in my sacrifice!"

The cover-up

The medical establishment knows that it has been withholding cures, and that this is now an existential threat to its legitimacy. We have seen unprecedented action by regulators in multiple countries to prevent the off-label use of HCQ for COVID-19. If there is a cheap and immediate cure, it removes the market for expensive patented drugs and exposes the con.

For example, in the USA the FDA has restricted its use to official clinical trials. To bring this to life, here is a quote from one American emergency room doctor:

> [Dr.] Dopko said in his 17 years of being a medical doctor, he has never seen the FDA issue restrictions on a drug like they have

> with hydroxychloroquine. "We've been told we're not supposed to prescribe hydroxychloroquine for Covid-19 unless the person is in the hospital and it's part of a clinical trial. I've never seen this before. Doctors prescribe drugs for off-label use all the time."

The same has happened in France, where HCQ was suspiciously reclassified as a "poisonous substance" on January 13, despite decades of safe use and being listed by WHO as an "essential medicine." Remember, denying people essential medical care is a crime against humanity: this was done by the same Macron government that has used illegal LBD40 ammunition against civilian protestors in breach of the Geneva Convention.

The same also applies in the UK, where HCQ is not being promoted by the NHS as standard protocol; this means many are dying on ventilators or in nursing homes for no good reason. "Do not resuscitate" orders are being widely signed by the elderly, who are effectively being culled to pad the COVID-19 numbers and hide the overreaction. Yes, it's that bad.

We also hear awful stories coming out of New York from whistleblower nurses saying patients are being left to rot and die since they lack family as advocates due to isolation of COVID-19 wards. The CDC has been caught reclassifying deaths, as the scam becomes too obvious. What happened to all the people dying of other causes, including old age? Where did they go? Where's the public outcry at the obvious massaging of the death toll numbers?

The consequences

Given the scale of the impact of COVID-19 and the failure of the medical profession to contain it (despite having the tools), this could well spell the end of allopathic medicine and "pharmacide." The functional and integrative people are the future: we need to put nutrition, immune system function, and actual wellbeing back into the heart of healthcare.

Coronagate is the deliberate withholding of a cure for COVID-19. The exposure of massive medical fraud enabled by media collusion will likely follow from it, for it is likely not the only condition or treatment where this is the case. The entire regulatory framework for medicine and the licensing monopolies of practice will be under pressure like never before. Laws like the 1939 Cancer Act in the UK need to be repealed to allow for radical new approaches by new entrants. Pharma advertising to the public needs to end immediately so media companies are no longer conflicted by their paymasters.

This scandal dovetails into others like Spygate and the targeting of General Flynn by Barack Obama's FBI and DOJ holdovers. A corrupt media has covered up for a corrupt government, and neither could be brought to account (until now) due to a corrupt justice system. Many people — including Bill Gates and Dr. Fauci — need to answer for their actions in court. Those in the media who have knowingly connived to hype the threat while withholding information about a cure should face prison.

We do not know whether COVID-19 is natural or manmade, and if the latter whether its release was accidental or deliberate. To the extent that we have a good enough cure, it doesn't matter at this point; indeed, we may never know, as the truth could trigger WW3. COVID-19 is already the defining economic and social event of our lives, and Coronagate promises to be the defining governance scandal of modern history.

If we bring people to justice and truly learn the lessons from it, it will trigger a deep reform of our medical, media and government institutions. If those reforms are successful, Coronagate could be the scandal to end all scandals. That is the only worthy legacy of the unnecessary COVID-19 and lockdown death tolls.

The Wars of Perception of Heaven and Hell

August 8, 2020

Of all tyrannies, a tyranny sincerely exercised for the good of its victims may be the most oppressive.
— C.S. Lewis

IF EVIL GENIUS IS A THING, how can we know when we have been deceived? For surely no matter how careful we are, there will always be a Machiavellian scheme that leverages greater cunning and longer experience at subversion than we can comprehend. This is no theoretical question, for our world is presently riven by violently opposing paradigms of what is righteous.

Over the past few years I have had a chance to step back from ordinary corporate work and learn more about the underpinnings of our technocratic society and its power base — banking, media, academia and IT. On the surface of modernity we have Enlightenment values and scientific rationality. Yet when you take the cultural covers off, you find inside a war on objectivity — and a monumental power struggle to define reality itself.

The roots of the anti-enlightenment movement (to the extent that the Enlightenment was enlightened) are complex and diverse. A recurring theme is the influence of the Frankfurt School and its "critical theory" ideology. To oversimplify, this forces all societal phenomena to be seen through a lens of power and domination: conflict and hierarchy (rather than loving kindness and nurture) are implicitly the driving forces of economic and social life.

To say that these Frankfurt School philosophical underpinnings of Cultural Marxism are controversial would be to push the boundaries of understatement. Critical theory appears to me to be a psychopathic doctrine, embedding false assumptions about the sharing of resources, the absence of mutual care among strangers, and the presence of rigid social classes and binding affiliations. It dehumanizes us, seeing us only as members of oppressor vs oppressed classes.

Modern "intersectionalism" drives this anti-individualist model to its awful conclusion of atomized competing identity groups. To progress in the world you must align to the appropriate "righteous" labels and approved Progressive sources of social privilege. This is where our deepest problems creep in, for the need to transfer power from the (alleged) oppressor to the (perceived) oppressed becomes a (wicked and tyrannical) end in itself: *everyone* becomes oppressed by those (in government and corporations) who arbitrate power.

This manipulation of group power in turn usurps individual ethics and scientific rationality, with terrible consequences. Any technocratic intervention can be retrospectively justified just as long as it aligns to the suggested oppressor/oppressed parties. One needs only to declare someone to be a *victim* ("an elderly person caught COVID") and the state (acting as *rescuer*) can override the individual natural rights of any supposed *perpetrator* ("mandatory vaccination for all").

The dysfunctional victim/persecutor/rescuer dynamic then sustains itself, with the former perpetrator becoming the new victim ("vaccine injuries"), the former rescuer becoming the new perpetrator ("tyrants with needles"), inviting the former victim to become the new rescuer ("compensation campaign"). At every turn more power is accumulated by the (often hidden) rulers of the system, and less is held by the sovereign individual. Innate Common Law rights are slowly crushed.

☙

This (un)ethical doctrine of "socially just" power transfer is the basis of a new quasi-official religion: Scientism. This is a rigid set of approved beliefs about us and our place in the cosmos. (Scientism has some difficulty fully explaining the conscious scientist observer, but that's best not mentioned in polite company.) Experts in Scientism are anointed to produce evidence which justifies the predetermined actions of power acting in its own interests.

If you're *really* good at Scientism you might get a doctorate certificate to prove your lack of heresy and acceptance into the official mainstream. This reverence for authority is the opposite of true science; as Richard Feynman said, "Science is the belief in the ignorance of experts." Implicit in this is the right of *any* individual to challenge the empirical and logical grounding of our public policy choices. Scientism is Cultural Marxism clothed in empirical rationality, and it leads to "Fake Science."

The unwelcome false conclusions of Scientism (like "Climate Change") have to be sold to the unwilling and unwitting public; thus "Fake Science" is twinned with "Fake News." The real science of manipulation of human beliefs — call it PR or propaganda — leads us to the dark discipline of social engineering. Places like the Tavistock Institute stand accused of deeply unethical activities in support of a corrupt establishment in their creation of the modern media industry. We are endlessly marketed "scientific" schemes that lead us to our own doom.

Computers can automate the modification of individual belief. In the world of social media and artificial intelligence algorithms, we can deliberately generate unity — *or conflict* — as a matter of policy. If the whole basis of your psychopathic power system is oppressors vs oppressed, then conquest of the mind is its fuel, and engineered social division is its fire. The greater the atomization of the public realm, the more energy is expended by the public fighting among themselves, and the less ire is directed at their feudal, overlord class.

Humans are naturally loving and cooperative; we raise children and care for pets. In order to sustain difference and division (and the ruling power of the Cultural Marxists), the public has to instead be persuaded to buy into alternate realities and false righteousness to reverse their natural harmony. Up has to become down, black is swapped with white, and the signposts to Heaven and Hell are reversed. A shared reality encourages undesired cultural cohesion— and thus empiricism and objectivity become the enemies of the corrupt and powerful.

ఌ

It is not hard to get people to confuse fact and fiction — Orson Welles's 1938 *War of the Worlds* radio broadcasts prove this amply. Thus, we enter into a kind of "Plato's Cave Complex," with endlessly branching caverns. Each "room" projects its own "shadow war movie" to its audience seeking relief from "identity oppression." Those in the cave complex may understand they even have a choice of shadow plays to watch, but they are never given enough understanding to exit their subterranean captivity to the movie producers.

Indeed, in order to scale this spelunking system of social control you need to shift the baseline perception of the entire population over time. A total inversion of reality is needed, where — as George Orwell said — "War is Peace, Freedom is Slavery, and Ignorance is Strength." Indeed, sickness is health, and truth is a lie. I've had to admit to myself that "abortion is healthcare" falls into this category; death is objectively not life for the unborn, and is a breach of the Hippocratic Oath.

Only by re-engineering the baseline to be completely upside-down can you then create the endless "subjective virtual reality caves" by re-injecting selected parts of objective reality. Otherwise the "realities" are too close and constrained by limited divergence from a shared understanding, and the atomic division and conquest of society fails. As I understand it, this total inversion of right and wrong, fact and fiction, is the essence of the Satanic doctrine.

Each cave dweller thinks they live in The Truth™, clinging onto their small unique part of validated objectivity. Those in neighboring cave areas, telling rival narratives, are self-evidently deluded. Heaven is your own shadow play, and Hell is anyone who talks of exiting the cave complex: they are probably violent extremists and part of a cult!

Speaking of which, I recommend reading a rather superb essay found on the website ilPedante.org. Translated from Italian into English by Gulab Bara, *A Cult of Death* introduces the idea of a "false synecdoche" to describe a similar observation:

> …an expedient technique of manipulation of public opinion that utilizes the delivery not of false information exactly, but rather of selected details, which in the absence of all the rest come to represent the entirety of the matter at hand in the perception of the receivers.

We often see this dynamic play out in modern politics where the overriding need is to sustain a chosen power narrative, regardless of evidence to the contrary. The very concept of objectivity is redefined subjectively and subjugated to the need to maintain control via cultural division (aka "diversity"… of anything except belief).

A good example of this comes from the British MP Nadia Whittome, who flashes her Cultural Marxism membership credentials:

> We must not fetishize "debate" as though debate is itself an innocuous, neutral act. The very act of debate in these cases is an effective rollback of assumed equality and a foot in the door for doubt and hatred.

In this post-Enlightenment world of Cultural Marxism, facts are subservient to dogmas. Ideas cannot be contested independently of those who advocate them — and their identity and power position. Detached observation and objective assessment is a form of violence ("hatred") against those with the weaker argument.

We see this in even more extreme form in the USA, where in Seattle public workers have been sent on "undoing whiteness" training (my emphasis): "Internalized Racial Superiority" was defined by perfectionism, **individualism**, imposition, arrogance, paternalism, silence, **intellectualization**, control, violence, comfort, appropriation, cognitive dissonance, **objectivity** and "anti-blackness."

Conflict sells a provocative fear narrative, and the TV news offers just enough containment of their fear to give people safety to continue until the next news bulletin. To sustain the conflict agenda, the mass media needs division and frequently manufactures it where none existed. That most of the world is objectively peaceful and most humans are harmonious cannot be honestly communicated.

The corporate media is involved in a full-on war against objectivity at present, and they are not in the least bit ashamed of it. *The Atlantic* openly mocks data-driven decision making:

> The Facts Man gives it to you straight. With his college degree, with his top-quality résumé, with his insider knowledge, with his background in Euclidean something-or-other — sharpened by debating with the smartest people, who never went to school — here is what he has found. These are the data. These are more data. This. Is. It. Here's the inevitable conclusion. It's the only conclusion possible!

Salon tells you "Americans aren't yearning for more and better 'objectivity' in journalism":

> That's not a failure of "objectivity" by the mainstream media; that's a willful departure from reality by a large chunk of the population. If anything, it suggests to me that the mainstream media's "objectivity" hang-up has resulted in a failure to successfully champion the truth.

The media mogul owners of Plato's Cave Complex define what is real and objective; you in the audience are to accept it as a given, and it is not to be questioned. At best you are given an opportunity to relocate to an adjoining cavern with a false shadow narrative more to your personal taste.

ᔓ

The Frankfurt School's destructive War on Objectivity has run for over two centuries. We are now at the denouement of this philosophical invasion of civil society. Two critical events have come together right at this moment in history that force us to either halt it and live freely, or submit to it as serfs.

The first is the multitude of political "mega scandals" all breaking which involve the complicity of the mass media. Specifically, we know that President Obama and his leadership team spied on the incoming Trump administration and launched a coup attempt via multiple fabricated efforts (Steele Dossier/Russiagate, Ukraine/Impeachment Hoax).

General Flynn was also falsely accused of crimes, then pursued by a corrupt DOJ/FBI through a compromised court system, in order to prevent him taking up his appointed role — and revealing treasonous scandals like Uranium One and Irangate. This power grab is the biggest political crime (to date) in American history.

The second is the rollout of face mask mandates for an overblown pandemic that is already over due to herd immunity being easily reached. The economy is being shuttered, cultural activity suspended, and normal social life shattered. Occult rituals (distancing, washing, covering, mocking) are forced on the unwitting masses through fearmongering and corrupt medics and the media.

Yet Ivermectin, Budesonide, and Hydroxychloroquine have all proven to be adequate treatments for COVID-19, rendering it into a condition no more threatening than flu. Meanwhile, the pharmaceutical industry is desperate to roll out rushed vaccines with no long-term safety case in yet another transparent power (and money) grab. Combined with tens of thousands of elderly people being sent to their deaths in nursing homes, this is the biggest medical crime (to date) in American history.

In reality, both the Spygate and Coronagate scandals are just hints as to a superstorm of corruption revelations to come. The subjectivist "Fake News" and "Fake Science" have never before faced such a direct and existential challenge: the objective hard facts on both of these issues are all laid out for anyone with the eyes to see and ears to hear.

On both of these issues the large community of open-source researchers and citizen journalists have been on target for years — while the official authorities and news sources are now completely discredited. Some of us have escaped the Plato's Cave Complex "prison of the mind," seen the sunshine outside, and returned inside to alert the others!

All the division and bitterness over which *subjective* false projection was the "right" objective one was pointless and misdirected. None of them were: you have to follow the "exit" sign. Heaven is not a cavern in the media complex at all; it is the objective outdoors!

∽

Which brings us near to our conclusion: how do we enable a "mass jailbreak" from this Hellish nightmare of Cultural Marxism, socially engineered division, and the accelerating enslavement of humanity via medical totalitarianism? As C.S. Lewis suggests, the worst possible tyranny is one done for your own health, and it's right in our face at present — literally.

There are impending events that will inevitably occur in the real world that force many to reflect hard upon their perception of Heaven and Hell. This drives a newfound inquisitiveness to discern what is objective and grounded — given a growing understanding of how evil genius has long had a deceptive reign over us.

An answer to this question is found in the much-derided QAnon movement. Q gives us a philosophical tool to determine who is naively watching a "subjective shadow play" versus who is able to reflect upon their objective position inside a damp cave. For it only takes a casual glance to see how the mass media refuses to deal with the actual merits of the Q drops — and their auxiliary hard evidence of widespread criminality and media collusion and cover-up.

The QAnon phenomenon is positioned by the criminal media as an insane alternative sub-reality *within* their "Universe of The Official Narrative." Words like "fringe," "debunked" and "extreme" deter the ordinary person from even examining the data. The crux of the matter is an awfully specific taboo: there cannot *ever* be media discussion of the identity of Q. For, this is the philosophical point on which the whole Fake News/Fake Science subjective paradigm fails.

The moment you consider the identity of Q, you have to expand your "universe of discourse" to include the presence of a "projectionist" — and reflect upon *what* is a projected shadow vs the real world. The "Universe of The Official Narrative" is too small to consider this simple question: is there a "projectionist" in the room? This tells you it is not the "encompassing" narrative, but rather the "encompassed" one.

In other words, the lies and propaganda of "Fake News" and "Fake Science" — over issues like Trump and COVID — are fully explicable within the QAnon cosmology, but the reverse is not true. We have an objective question of fact — the identity of Q — which creates a philosophical instrument to tell whose cosmology is "the cave" and whose is "just shadows."

The news is fake, the war (on objectivity) is real. The endless subjection of the public to false narratives they perceive as genuine is smashed by the Q "information bunker buster." It is a precision weapon to locate and destroy the "projectors" of faked reality — no matter how deeply they are buried.

There's a heavenly irony to the end of hellish Cultural Marxism resting on a simple identity question.

Benevolent genius, indeed.

ೞ

The Digital Coup and the Great Exposure

November 27, 2020

THIS CHAPTER IS NOT MEANT FOR YOU. No, really, it isn't. Especially if you are a subscriber to my newsletter. Nearly all the subscribers on my newsletter mailing list don't need to read it. And those who do need to won't read it.

Yet.

But they soon will. Over and over.

Let me explain.

In the next few weeks, the awful truth about the recent US election and the attempted theft of the Presidency from the People will become impossible to ignore. The Director of National Intelligence is tasked with delivering his assessment of the integrity of the election within 45 days — the deadline being December 18th. Other lawsuits and events are progressing in the interim.

We are already witnessing the run-up to the disclosure of fraud and foreign interference prior to the December 14th electoral college vote. Fraud vitiates everything and annuls the Biden candidacy; foreign interference makes this a matter of military law. You are going to see a mass treason event and huge numbers of people brought to justice. This wasn't really an election; it was a military intelligence sting operation against a corrupt establishment.

There are significant objective reasons to believe that this election was NOT won legitimately by Joe Biden:

The candidate — Joe Biden had previously stood for the Presidency, found to be a liar about his past, and self-declared himself unfit for the role on national TV. Uncharismatic, Joe has had few notable achievements, and is liable to fondle children in public — not qualities that endear you to the masses. Furthermore, he had a miasma of corruption around him linked to both China and Ukraine.

The party — The Democratic party alienated large swathes of its traditional base through support for violent uprisings in cities it controlled (via BLM and Antifa), conducted with the tacit approval of its leaders. Failed attempts to unseat Donald Trump ("Russian Collusion" damp squib and Impeachment failure) damaged its reputation for political competence.

The campaign — Donald Trump repeatedly filled arenas and generated wild enthusiasm from his supporters with his rallies, whereas Joe Biden was notoriously unable to summon crowds. He essentially abandoned campaigning during the last ten days and demonstrated incredibly low levels of energy and poor mental focus in his speeches.

The process — The Dominion voting machines were not under the control of Americans, and their own manuals and processes demonstrate extremely poor security and features to manually manipulate votes. The synchronized halting of counting in key states and the sudden "discovery" of huge numbers of Biden votes are automatically cause for alarm. More votes were counted than the machines could process in the time available.

The outcome — There are many staggering anomalies in the outcome — including the tiny number of counties won, the weird geographical distribution of cities won, the unprecedented size of the Biden vote (especially compared to Obama), Trump "losing" despite raising his vote, the implausible total support for Biden from military votes, and the contradiction of the Presidency (Democratic) with the House vote (Republican seats all held).

The investigation — We are already seeing large numbers of affidavits sworn that testify to fraud, video evidence of ballots being mishandled and destroyed, large irregularities in following the lawful processes of the election, and obvious failures to pass basic statistical tests for legitimacy (like Benford's Law).

The justice — President Trump issued a specific executive order on September 12, 2018, in anticipation of this election and the need to expose all the corruption in the civilian justice system, as well as the illegitimacy of many past elections in the USA and worldwide. (Find "Executive Order on Imposing Certain Sanctions in the Event of Foreign Interference in a United States Election" on whitehouse.gov.) All the clues are there for those with the eyes to see of a highly managed and planned process. This includes the expanded means for delivering the death penalty for treason.

The unavoidable picture that is emerging is one of a Digital Coup. The rogue intelligence agencies in the US and elsewhere had perfected a toolkit for "color revolutions." This included sophisticated election hacking, designed to deliver the desired result in a highly plausible manner. The Dominion voting solution was not for vote counting, but for election fraud — by design.

These tools were deployed against the US population in an illegal act of war. There is evidence of involvement by both China and Iran; other powers may also be exposed, including supposed allies, if the Russiagate precedent tells us anything. The enormous Trump landslide was outside of the range the fraud systems were configured for, which caused a panic insertion of fake paper ballots and extreme and obvious levels of digital "vote switching."

❧

I get to watch various tech industry email discussion lists and WhatsApp groups. These are overwhelmingly dominated by Biden voters. They are currently in a bubble disconnected from the reality of events past and present. This bubble is about to burst. Many of their political idols will be executed for treason, or spend life in prison for sedition. There is wisdom in advice not to worship idols.

For my tech industry associates, you need to understand that the controlled mass media is gaslighting you and deliberately pushing a desperate false narrative to cover for their own criminality. They say, "no evidence of fraud" and "unsubstantiated" allegations, even as that **hard evidence**

mounts up in court filings and open-source intelligence analysis. There are districts with more votes than voters, yet you believe self-evident lies from your TV.

You have been hoodwinked by a system of social engineering that was covertly established, mainly after the 1963 *de facto* coup following the assassination of President Kennedy, and installation of a permanent criminal shadow government.

Today, Biden voters are celebrating his being the media's "President-elect" (hint: the media has no constitutional role in elections); the funding of his transition (hint: another sting operation); and Trump's imminent departure from the White House (hint: he has planned this operation for decades and isn't going anywhere). My former tech industry associates are utterly delusional in their beliefs.

There is absolutely no way that the US military would have spent years tangibly preparing us for this watershed event, including bringing Trump into the Presidency, only to allow assets of the Chinese Communist Party to (re)take control over the United States of America. It just isn't happening. These celebrations will be short-lived as the "boomerang" motion of the vast sting operation becomes unmistakable and unavoidable.

∽

If you voted for Joe Biden and are trying to make sense of dislocating events unfolding fast, here is where you have gone wrong.

Firstly, you have excluded from your inputs all rival voices and competing sources of information. You have immersed yourself in a narcissistic culture of self-congratulatory, presumed superiority based on egotistical intellectual achievement. By the time you read this, you will be witnessing that belief system crashing and burning: pride smashed by the fall. You drove out the diversity that mattered, which was a diversity of opinion and social understanding. You were intolerant of dissent, and tolerant of censorship. This will remain a stain upon your conscience and reputation until you respect those who saw the criminality and spoke out.

Secondly, you have failed to understand the nature of propaganda and how clever, intellectual people are the MOST susceptible, not the LEAST. You NEED propaganda in order to have a socially acceptable position on each issue; nobody has time to become a climate scientist, vaccine safety expert, and forensic accountant and research every controversy. You have treated different media outlets as independent sources when in reality they are all one (false) voice. You are a victim of pervasive propaganda and even mind control.

Thirdly, you have abandoned objective rational empirical inquiry. You have assumed that (local social) consensus is rationality, and deviation from that consensus is madness — a cult even. You have ridiculed and mocked those who chose to look at the data — ALL THE DATA — and then made up their mind ONLY based on where it directed them, and not their preconception of what was thinkable or acceptable. This is the basis of **proper science** and requires humility to recognize that progress is made by **admitting errors** and **reversing false beliefs**.

∽

I looked at ALL the data in this case and changed my beliefs. You DID NOT and stayed the same. This is why you have FAILED this test of sanity. Such failure needs to be confronted — because your false beliefs are **dangerous to us all** since they perpetuate evil. The "short cut" the media (and academia) offered you was to a labyrinth of lies by assets of a criminal ruling class. You swallowed their lies willingly.

It was previously always easy to find a justification for your beliefs, another propaganda "talking point" to counter any data offered. A sneering and condescending attitude let you easily dismiss legitimate concerns as "extremist" or "conspiracy theories." By the time you read this, that's all finished. Gone. Over.

That you have been attacked by a ruthless, transnational "supermafia" armed with weaponized psychology and a whole media industry is not your fault. That others had life experiences or innate character that brought them to question the "official narrative" more quickly is also not their personal virtue. You are not my enemy, and I am not yours. Our job is to come together, respectfully and responsibly, so that we may realign and heal.

For those who were deceived by the grand illusions on offer, you will find that those at whom you laughed will most likely welcome you back with open arms. The precondition is that you respect equality under the rule of law and cease to put yourself on a pedestal where you are part of a superior social class entitled to judge others and look down upon them. It is time for you to be held to your stated values of kindness, tolerance, and inclusion.

For, we all have a real war to fight against a real enemy who can do us real harm. A war of infiltration, founded on treachery, that has corroded and corrupted our society. A war against great deceptions that fuel endless violent conflict.

The Great Exposure has begun. It cannot be stopped by anybody. Lasting peace is our goal and prize.

Please unify with those who are already fighting for truth and justice.

ഗ

About the Author

MARTIN GEDDES is a "professional polymath." His parents gave him a computer at around the age of 11, and that was the last they saw of him, for he disappeared into his bedroom. Having collected a degree in Mathematics and Computation from the University of Oxford, he then spent the 1990s building banking systems and doing IT consulting.

A move to Kansas in 2001 led to three years of exploring the American heartland, as well as experiencing the tragic changes surrounding the events of September 11 that year. His concomitant switch from IT to telecoms opened up a new career as a guru on the future of the internet. This included pioneering work on network performance science, and he became co-founder of the Hypervoice Consortium.

A growing sense of unease with the state of the world led Martin to explore the world of "conspiracy theories," only to find that the "official" story on many events was implausible or absurd. Martin applied his professional skill — dismantling belief systems to find their disconnects — to the domain of world affairs and corruption. As a result, his focus shifted from esoteric internet architecture and policy issues to mainstream concerns about privacy and corruption.

By coincidence, the Q phenomenon arrived at the same time, and intellectual rigor was widely valued and appreciated. As a result, Martin has become one of the leading authorities on the unfolding "silent war" against mass media propaganda, corrupt intelligence agencies, and secret societies.

As a by-product of becoming a whistleblower on criminality in the media and tech world, he was ostracized by colleagues and associates. Isolation led to an unanticipated new career as a photographic artist. His small army of Twitter followers have become enthusiastic consumers of his daily "photo walks" —through which Martin has become a one-man "psyop" for the cause of finding beauty in the ordinary.

He has two teenage daughters, lives in London, and is out and proud.